Holocaust's Child

TEN STORIES OF CHILDREN WHO SURVIVED

AMY and W. R. BLOCHER

Mechanicsburg, PA USA

Published by Sunbury Press, Inc.
Mechanicsburg, Pennsylvania

www.sunburypress.com

ISBN: 978-1-62006-135-0 (Trade Paperback)

Library of Congress Control Number: Application in Process

FIRST SUNBURY PRESS EDITION: May 2019

Product of the United States of America
0 1 1 2 3 5 8 13 21 34 55

Set in Bookman Old Style
Designed by Crystal Devine
Cover by Terry Kennedy
Edited by Lawrence Knorr

Continue the Enlightenment!

This book is dedicated to the six million victims and the survivors of the Holocaust, may their memories never fade, and to the Righteous Gentiles, both those known to us and those known only to God, who risked their lives, and sometimes died, to save the victims of murderous anti-Semitism.

CONTENTS

FOREWORD

Someone asked me if I was going to have a famous person write a foreword to this book.

I said no.

I had two reasons for that response. The first one is that I don't know anyone famous.

But the second reason would have made the lack of a famous acquaintance irrelevant: I wanted to say something that someone else couldn't.

Primarily it is this: This book is the product of a dream my wife has had for many decades to contribute to the store of memories from survivors of the Holocaust so that the world will never forget what happened.

Amy taught middle and high school for 37 years, mostly as an English teacher. Her lessons included teaching about the Holocaust. She also taught about the Holocaust in Sunday school and to others outside of school.

When she retired at age 62, she started searching for ways to make her dream a reality. She first turned to our daughter, Jyssica Schwartz, to work with her as co-author. Jyssica is an excellent freelance writer who had published two books and was working on a third, along with a host of other projects. Finding the time to devote to the kind of project her mother envisioned just wasn't possible for her.

Then I retired at the age of 67 after 41 years as a journalist, working mostly as an editor at small and medium-sized newspapers.

One day in late 2017, shortly after I retired, Amy and I were running errands. While I was driving, she was on the phone with Jyssica talking about this book. As Jyssica explained to her mother that she lacked the time, our daughter pointed out that Amy was sitting next to someone who not only had the time but also the skills to work with her.

That is how I became involved. And more than a year later, we have completed this book. It has been a journey of passion, sadness, and survival. As you read this book, I hope you see these survivors' persistence, their journeys and the hope they held onto. Without hope, none of us would be here. The true overarching thread in this book remains hope and survival—and not just surviving, but thriving, in the aftermath of horror.

We would like to thank Lawrence Knorr, publisher of Sunbury Press, and his team for their help in producing this book and truly making it a reality.

We would also like to thank Jyssica for her invaluable help in editing and organizing this book, and for acting as our agent in securing a publisher. She had the experience in that area we both lacked.

And we would like to thank our son, Charlie Blocher, for his valuable comments which helped in the writing.

Most of all we would like to thank the ten survivors who so generously opened their homes and their lives to us. Without their generosity, this book would not have been possible.

— W.R. Blocher

CHAPTER 1

WHY?

Never again.

This became the mantra for Jews following the Holocaust.

To understand why requires knowing what happened and why it happened.

What follows are the stories of ten children who survived this horror. These children of the Holocaust ranged in age from just three years old to young teens when their experience with the Holocaust began. Some survived the camps and ghettos. Some survived by hiding, at times with the help of non-Jews who risked their lives to help. Some survived by running east into the Soviet Union, staying ahead of the advancing Germans.

But their lives did not begin with the Holocaust or end with World War II. To gain a fuller understanding of what their experiences meant to them, their stories start, in all but one case, before the war. That one case involves a baby who was born after the war started and whose mother threw her over the concentration camp's barbed-wire fence in the desperate hope that her three-year-old daughter would survive. Their stories continue after the war as they rebuilt their shattered lives.

Their lives also were not lived in isolation from the world. With that in mind, each of these ten stories is told in the context of what was happening around them. Each of these stories was written to stand on its own. But they also build on each other, providing a fuller understanding of the range of experiences during the Holocaust, since each of the ten found different ways of surviving–some by their own wits, some by the efforts of their parents and others, some by a combination of all of them.

They are among the remnant of the more than six million Jews who fell under Nazi domination.

—

About 9.5 million Jews, sixty percent of the world's Jewish population, lived in Europe before the Holocaust, mostly in Eastern Europe. But all those millions of Jews made up just 1.7 percent of Europe's population. The heaviest Jewish concentration was in Poland where three million Jews were 9.5 percent of that country's population. The next heaviest concentration of Jews was in the Soviet Union, where 2.52 million lived, making up 3.4 percent of the population. In western Europe, only in the Netherlands was the Jewish population–156,000–more than one percent of the population.[1]

Germany was home to only about 525,000 Jews, 0.75 of one percent of the population.

If the Nazis had had their way, none of those 9.5 million Jews would have survived the war. As it was, the Germans and the other Europeans who cooperated with them, murdered six million children, women, and men. Young and old. Sick and healthy.

Some were gassed.

Some were shot.

Some beaten to death.

Some worked to death.

Some starved to death.

Some, weakened by starvation and the lack of medical care, died of disease.

Some suffocated in tightly packed cattle cars on their way to extermination camps.

Some were murdered on death marches if they didn't freeze to death along the way or while being transported west in open cars during the winter to keep them out of the hands of the advancing Soviet Red Army as Germany's armed forces crumbled in both the east and west.

The murder machine was finally stopped when Germany was crushed between the American and British armies striking from the west and the Soviet Red Army attacking from the east.

—

While hatred of Jews is ancient, the term "anti-Semitism" is a modern invention. The word was coined in 1879 by Wilhelm Marr, a German journalist who wanted a term to define the hatred of Jews, as well as hatred of various trends associated with Jews in the eighteenth and nineteenth centuries, such as equal civil rights, constitutional democracy, free trade, socialism, finance capitalism, and pacifism.[2]

The roots of anti-Semitism can be found in the ancient world. The Holocaust was simply its most horrendous manifestation. Despite so few Jews living in Germany, or in the rest of Europe, Jews were accused of being enemies of the nation and of civilization itself.

Europe's Jews fell victim to three human traits. Hatred of the other and ideology are linked with ideology was put in service of hatred. The third was political expedience when rulers used Jews as scapegoats to divert their populations' attention away from their own blunders and shortcomings.

That ideology of hatred has been building for millennia. In the third century BCE, an Egyptian priest named Manetho claimed the Israelites were a race of lepers who were thrown out of Egypt, not led out by Moses. Greek and Egyptian scholars of the time portrayed Jewish culture as sterile, and Jews as "godless" people who worshiped an ass's head in the Jerusalem Temple. They also produced the first blood libel, claiming Jews would kidnap a Greek whom they then fed to their deity in the Holy of Holies. They also attacked the Jews for not assimilating and for hating the gods.[3]

Then there was the problem of success. In Alexandria, Egypt, Jews made up about 40 percent of that cosmopolitan center's population. The pagan population resented them because of their commercial success, their equal rights, and their special religious privileges which allowed them to worship just their God, and not the gods of all the others.[4]

In the fourth century CE, Christianity became the official religion of the Roman Empire, and Jews lost the privileges they had under the pagan empire. Rabbis were stripped of their authority, Jewish proselytism and sexual relations with Christian women were crimes invoking death sentences. Jews were also banned from the military and high office.[5]

In Europe, the growth of Christian feudal society following the Western Roman Empire's collapse squeezed Jews out of economic life. Jews couldn't own land because they couldn't take the required Christian oaths. The formation of merchants' guilds, which controlled international commerce, excluded Jews. Many Jews were driven into poverty. Those who had money became money lenders as the only way left to make a living, something Christian religious authorities at the time allowed because they banned lending money for interest between Christians. This financing was needed by the expanding trade, as well as nobles and churchmen in need of money to support their lifestyles, and monarchs who were expanding their governments and waging war.[6]

Jewish lenders would charge interest rates as high as fifty percent because it was difficult for them to recoup their loans since they were not allowed to go to court to collect. They were fortunate if they could collect on half the loans they made. Non-Jewish lenders, despite the church's ban, charged comparable rates.[7]

At the time of the First Crusade at the end of the eleventh century, Jews faced murderous violence. As the crusaders started their journey toward Jerusalem, they first turned on the Jews of France and then in the Rhineland. Pogroms began as early as December 1095 in Rouen, France, prompting those Jews to warn the German communities. Led by aristocrats, these crusaders attacked the Jewish communities along the Rhine River, with the worst attacks coming at Mainz and Worms.[8]

In Worms, nearly the entire Jewish community–men, women, and children–was wiped out by May 20, 1096. Jews were either killed outright or after refusing forced conversion to Christianity. Five days later at Mainz, the crusaders killed the 700 Jewish men who fought them and then went on to kill women and children. The Mainz Jews had sought the protection of the city's archbishop since the Catholic Church opposed forced conversion and murder. Albert of Aachen agreed to provide protection after the payment of what he called an "incredible amount of money," but did little to help them.[9]

The Blood Libel, in which Jews were accused of committing ritual murder, has its origins in Norwich, England, when a Christian boy was murdered just before Easter in 1144. Despite having no evidence, the local Jews were blamed on the belief that they wanted to mock the crucifixion of Jesus. The boy was soon considered Europe's first child martyr. The Blood Libel soon spread throughout England and Europe.[10]

In 1215, the Catholic Church's Fourth Lateran Council decreed Jews should live in ghettos and wear a yellow label on their clothes to identify them,[11] but it wasn't until 1516 that the first official ghetto was created in Venice. While the origin of the term is in dispute, the result is not. Jews were forced to live in a walled-in area, with armed men at the entrances to enforce a curfew. The practice spread throughout Europe in the sixteenth and seventeenth centuries.[12]

Perhaps the most famous, although not the first, expulsion of Jews came in 1492 when, after conquering the last Moslem-held territory on the Iberian Peninsula, King Ferdinand and Queen Isabella of Spain forced Jews to either emigrate or convert. The expulsion followed a long history of violence against Jews, even though earlier rulers had been tolerant of them. Some Jews had become increasingly part of Spanish society, including acting as councilors and physicians for the kings of Castile and Aragon. This provoked the animosity of nobles and common people, as well as churchmen who saw this an insult to Christianity. In 1391, for instance, a mob in Seville invaded the Jewish quarter, murdering 4,000 people. The violence spread to other areas of Spain, and within three months about 50,000 Jews were dead and more than that had undergone forced baptism.[13]

But conversion did not mean acceptance. The Spanish called the baptized Jews "New Christians"–or "marranos," pigs. The New Christians faced the same stereotypes their Jewish ancestors had because their blood was considered tainted. Old Christian blood was considered pure.[14]

As Europe moved into the Renaissance and beyond, anti-Semitism did not ease, even though Jews were gradually emancipated, gaining citizenship, civil rights, and being allowed to live outside ghettos. At the dawn of the nineteenth century, Napoleon Bonaparte made Jews French citizens. And Jews were emancipated where French armies occupied areas in western and central Europe.[15]

In the Russian Empire, most Jews were confined to what became known as the Pale of Settlement on the western fringe of the empire. The Tsarist government wanted to prevent Jews from competing commercially in the interior of Russia and found Jews were convenient scapegoats for economic troubles.[16] Attacks on Jewish communities were a continuing threat. In 1881, for instance, pogroms hit 160 cities and villages, with no attempt by the government to intervene.[17]

A Russian Tsarist official was responsible for creating "The Protocols of the Elders of Zion," an anti-Semitic pamphlet, in 1897 or 1898. The pamphlet purports to contain the minutes of a secret meeting among Jewish sages who were plotting to control the world. As a result of the false accusations, Jews were blamed for past and present disasters, the destruction of Christian monarchies, and promoting liberal ideas. "The Protocols" were published in Russia in 1903 and spread throughout Europe and the rest of the world.[18]

Even though in 1921 The Times of London proved "The Protocols" was fake, the work is accepted today as fact by anti-Semites and is taught as fact in many textbooks in the Arab and Islamic world.[19]

The Nazis simply gave this anti-Semitism its most murderous form, with murder organized on an industrial scale. The Nazi ideology, drawing on some non-German pseudo-science sources, held Jews to be sub-humans who were undermining European civilization and weakening the pure Aryan blood of the master race. They and the other anti-Semites who bought into this belief made this their "reality." They justified their murderous actions based on this fiction.

Jews were accused of dominating the capitalist system through banking and other means, and after Communism came along, of being communists, regardless of their political or religious beliefs.

And the Nazis and other Germans accused Jews of being major players in the mythical Stab in the Back–the fiction that in World War I, the German army was not defeated in the field, rather the blame was put on traitors at home who undermined the army and forced the armistice. This charge was made despite all the evidence to the contrary. Germany was exhausted after four years of war. Its army was not only facing the French and the British, but a fresh American Army. The German army was suffering major defeats and was in retreat.

During the Depression, after Adolf Hitler rose to power in Germany in 1933, the Nazis laid the blame for the nation's economic woes on Jews. Over the next few years, Jews were forced out of government jobs, out of the legal system, medicine, and other professions, out of teaching in universities and schools, out of the arts, out of business, and were deprived of their German citizenship, stripping them of their civil rights. Their children could not attend public schools. Jews could not go to public parks. And when Jews wanted to emigrate, the Nazis made them pay for that privilege.

—

After Germany's defeat, Jews were still being killed in Eastern Europe. Sometimes Jews were killed by Christians who had claimed the Jews' property after they were deported and didn't want to return what they had stolen. At other times, Jews were killed simply because they were Jews. The war had unleashed anti-Semitism, and there were Eastern Europeans who just kept on killing Jews.

Following World War II, anti-Semitism in the West took a bit of a breather, although it would take years before some forms of discrimination against Jews ended, such as limits by some universities on the number of Jews who would be admitted.

And while violence against Jews is mainly coming from the right, the extreme left is also delving into anti-Semitism. The Boycott, Divestment, Sanctions [BDS] movement, popular among some academics and university students in Western Europe and the United States, sells itself as a movement which "works to end international support of Israel's oppression of Palestinians and to pressure Israel to comply with international law."[20]

Since being anti-Semitic has become unfashionable on the left, being anti-Israel has replaced it. The intent is the same, just the name is different. The BDS proponents show an ignorance, perhaps a willful ignorance, of the history of the Mideast and of the current conditions there.

Anti-Semitism has been growing steadily in Europe, where Jews and Jewish communities have been targeted, and it is taught in many schools in the Moslem world. The BDS movement is thriving in Europe, and right-wing groups are preaching anti-Semitism.

With such hate on the rise, the declaration "Never Again" perhaps should be reformulated–as a question:

Never Again?

Not without a fight.

Not without a fight.

NOTES

1. The Holocaust Encyclopedia, https://encyclopedia.ushmm.org.
2. The Holocaust Encyclopedia.
3. Robert S. Wistrich, *Antisemitism: The Longest Hatred* (n.p.: Panetheon Books, 1991): 5.
4. Wistrich, *Antisemitism: The Longest Hatred,* 6.
5. Wistrich, *Antisemitism: The Longest Hatred,* 4.
6. Norman C. Cantor, *The Civilization of the Middle Ages* (n.p.: HarperCollins, 1993): 365.
7. Cantor, *The Civilization of the Middle Ages,* 365.
8. Thomas Asbridge, *The First Crusade* (n.p. Oxford University Press, 2004): 84–85.
9. Asbridge, *The First Crusade,* 88.
10. Cantor, *The Civilization of the Middle Ages,* 366.
11. Jewish World, Haaretz.com.
12. Wistrich, *Antisemitism: The Longest Hatred,* 30–31.
13. Wistrich, *Antisemitism: The Longest Hatred,* 35–36.
14. Wistrich, *Antisemitism: The Longest Hatred,* 36–37.
15. Jewish Virtual Library, https://www.jewishvirtuallibrary.org.
16. Jewish Virtual Library.
17. Wistrich, *Antisemitism: The Longest Hatred,* 172–173.
18. My Jewish Learning, https://www.myjewishlearning.com.
19. The Holocaust Encyclopedia.
20. bds.movement.net.

"I believe always I have to be alive and see the family. I say, 'God help me.' I was praying every day to be alive."

—Miriam Apfel

CHAPTER 2

REFUSING TO GIVE UP

Miriam Apfel, formerly Miriam Levental

When Bracha Levental found out children considered too young to work were being deported by the Nazi invaders to their deaths, she protected her five daughters who were still living at home by getting them new birth certificates.

Her youngest, thirteen-year-old Miriam, would suddenly become fifteen. Living under Nazi rule, the young teenager acted even older, showing chutzpah and courage, and thinking quickly on her feet. Because of that, she was able to save not only herself but the lives of a number of other Jews, including her brother.

Miriam, like her five older sisters and her brother, was born in Piatza, Poland, near Krakow. Her birthday was May 6, 1926, although thirteen years later, her official date of birth would become May 6, 1924.

In 1927, when Miriam was one year old, her father, Mottel Levental, and her mother decided to move their family to Sosnowiec, which was about 52 miles northwest of Krakow, because they wanted their children to grow up with *Yiddishkeit*—learning a

Jewish way of life and customs. Sosnowiec, with a population of approximately 130,000, was home to about 28,000 Jews.[1] That was a large enough population to support Jewish schools, including a high school and vocational schools.

"The parents wanted us to grow up in a bigger city and have . . . better schools."

Mottel Levental supported his family by working as a salesman providing material for suits and coats to stores, while her mother created a home for their seven children. The family lived in an apartment in a three-story building with mostly other Jewish families, although a few Poles lived there as well. Mylech was the couple's only son and the oldest, having been born in 1911. Their six daughters followed: Regina in 1913, Pola in 1915, Adeaa in 1917, Nadja in 1919, Frimka in 1924, and finally Miriam, two years later.

The four eldest children were born in the Austro-Hungarian Empire, while the three youngest were born after it fell apart following Hungary's withdrawal on October 31, 1918, as Germany and its allies, Austro-Hungary and Turkey, were facing defeat at the end of World War I. Three days before Hungary had withdrawn, Czechoslovakia had declared its independence from the empire, followed a day later on October 29 by the South Slavs.[2] The Austro-Hungarians left the war eleven days before Germany, signing an armistice on November 3, 1918, with Italy, which was fighting with the British and French. A major defeat to the Italians on October 24 was the final blow for Austrians.[3]

Following the armistice that ended World War I, Poland regained its independence after 123 years of being sliced up by Austria, Russia, and Germany.[4] The Poles marked their independence on Armistice Day, November 11, 1918, when Warsaw's German garrison turned over its arms and strategic locations to Polish troops, mostly without violence, and evacuated the city, returning to Germany.[5]

By 1939, Miriam's brother, Mylech, had married and had one child. Her oldest sister, Regina, was also married and had two children. Pola and Adeaa were working in a chocolate factory, while Nadja was working in a clothing factory sewing men's shirts. Miriam was in the sixth grade, and Frimka was also in school.

Sosnowiec was in Upper Silesia, an area rich in coal and iron, which supported related industries. However, the Polish government limited Jewish employment in those businesses. To make

Miriam is second from the left with the school mascot under her left arm in the photograph that was taken about 1937. (Courtesy of Miriam Apfel.)

a living, many Jews were involved in commercial businesses and crafts.[6]

Poland of 1939 was a country under threat. Germany proper was to its west and East Prussia was on its north. The Treaty of Versailles had given Poland access to the Baltic Sea through what was called the Polish Corridor, which split Germany. Inside the corridor was Danzig, a coastal city with a population dominated by Germans. The corridor itself had a mixed population of Germans and Poles.[7] To the south of Poland lay what was left of Czechoslovakia, which had been occupied by the Germans in 1938. To the east was the Soviet Union, which had fought a border war with Poland about 1920. Poland also had a short border with Romania in the southeast.

German Führer Adolf Hitler demanded Poland return Danzig to Germany and allow extraterritorial access to the city.[8] The

Miriam, left, is with her oldest sister, Regina, and Regina's son, Asher, about 1938. (Courtesy of Miriam Apfel.)

Nazi leader based his demand on a desire to bring all Germans into the borders of the Reich, the same rationale he used when he successfully won British and French agreement to annex the Czech Sudetenland in October 1938, which led to that country's occupation by the Nazis.

The Poles rejected the German demand, relying in part on its treaties with Britain and France to deter German aggression.

In his plans to destroy Poland, Hitler believed the British and French would stay out of the war, a belief which was in practice justified. He also wanted to keep the Soviets out of the war at this point. Just before the invasion of Poland, the Germans and the Soviets signed a nonaggression pact on August 23, 1939. The treaty included a secret protocol calling for the dismemberment of Poland.[9]

With that assurance in hand, the Wehrmacht, the German armed forces, launched its invasion on September 1, 1939, with forces crossing the Polish border from the west, north, and south. Britain and France declared war on September 3, after their ultimatum for a German withdrawal was ignored.

While the British guarantee to Poland made no specific promises, the French had promised to launch major military actions against the Germans soon after a war started. Yet General Maurice Gamelin, commander of the French army, had told his government a major offensive could not be launched in fewer than two years.[10]

As Poland was being destroyed, the French, who had mobilized, stayed behind their defenses and watched. The British had 158,000 men in France by October 11, three weeks after the death of Poland.[11]

German soldiers reached Sosnowiec three days after the war started. As the fighting neared, with the Germans dropping bombs and people being killed, Jews and Poles fled. Mottel led his family east toward the comparative safety of Olkusz, in southeast Poland. Adeaa's boyfriend, Zalman, refused to go with the family, opting to stay with his parents and assuring her he would be safe once the German soldiers had passed through.

By September 17, the fighting was essentially over. The remnants of the Polish army were either surrounded by the Germans or had been pushed to the extreme east of the country along the Soviet border.[12] It was then that the Red Army invaded, taking a slice of Poland under the agreement with the Germans and murdering the Polish officers it captured. Some Polish troops managed to escape through Rumania, eventually joining the British and French in the fight against Germany. Some were able to fight with the British following the fall of France in June 1940.

As the fighting ended, the Leventals headed back to their homes in Sosnowiec. Their first encounter with German soldiers was a bloody one. As they were crossing a bridge with other Jews, the Germans started yelling at them and throwing some Jewish men and boys into the river below. Some drowned. Others were shot as they tried to swim to safety.

When they reached Sosnowiec, the city's Jews were tense and agitated. Miriam and her family were told all Jewish men and boys from age fourteen and older had been shot. They were told

Zalman, Adeaa's boyfriend, was among those who were buried in a mass grave.

But a living Zalman eventually showed up at their door. He had laid in the mass grave, pretending to be dead, for three days and then went into hiding for two more days, before going to Regina's home because he was afraid to return to his own.

Under Nazi occupation, life changed drastically for the Jews in Sosnowiec. The city's synagogue was burned and Jews were ordered to wear the Star of David.[13] Jewish schools were closed.

In 1939, Jewish men were being taken to work camps, including Miriam's brother, Mylech, who eventually went to the Markstadt forced labor camp, which was set up for Alfred Krupp's artillery factory in 1940.[14]

Next, the *Judenrat*, or Jewish Council, came for Regina's husband, Moshe, and Zalman, under orders from the Germans to provide workers. Both joined the rush by Jewish men to the comparative safety of the Soviet Union. After Moshe crossed the border, he wrote to Regina, telling her to sell everything in the house and run for the border with their two children, three-year-old Asher and eight-month-old Leah.

"She sold everything in the house, she came to us, she wanted to run. My mother and father said, 'How can you run with two kids?'"

But since she was determined to do just that, their parents told Adeaa and Nadja, "Go with her to the border and come back." The border was open when they reached it, allowing them to cross into what had become the Soviet Union. "When they want to go back, the border was closed, so they stayed in Russia."

In October 1939, Sosnowiec was made a part of Germany, along with other areas of the border, some of which had been in Germany prior to World War I, and transferred to Poland in 1918, and others which had not.[15] Sosnowiec reverted to its German name, Sosnowitz.[16]

In late October 1939, the Nazis appointed Moshe Merin to oversee the Jewish communities in Eastern Upper Silesia, which contained Sosnowiec and Bedzin, which together had a Jewish population of about 50,000. Including the small villages in his territory, Merin ruled over approximately 100,000 Jews.[17]

Merin has been accused of having a dictatorial style and of being willing to work with the Germans in order to maintain his power. He represented all the Jewish councils in the area to the

Miriam's parents, Bracha and Mottel Levental. (Courtesy of Miriam Apfel.)

Germans and could change their membership at will, which he did if the chairman and council members did not follow his orders. Those who resisted were either replaced or simply disappeared.[18] But he is also credited with keeping the mortality rate in his area lower than it was before the war.[19]

To fill the German quota for forced laborers, Merin and his Central Committee first used a volunteer system to funnel young men to work in Germany or Eastern Upper Silesia. But as word spread about the conditions in the labor camps, men stopped volunteering. So Merin instituted conscription, using coercion when needed, including threats to children and parents. Jewish police brought conscripts to assembly points if they would not report on their own. Conscripts and their families were allowed to pay ransom to Merin to escape forced labor. But the payment was no guarantee—the conscript might be shipped out anyway.[20]

As in other areas, the Germans confiscated Jewish property and set up workshops, producing such things as shoes and textiles. The Jews who worked in those shops felt safe from being deported for forced labor.[21]

The Germans had no use for children they considered too young to work, so they killed them. That's when Bracha Levental decided her daughters had to age two years. Since Regina was not only out of the house but out of the country, she moved her birth

Miriam's sister Pola. (Courtesy of Miriam Apfel.)

certificate to the next older and so on down the line, aging all her daughters by two years. That is how Miriam's birthday moved from 1926 to 1924, and the petite four-foot-six, blond, blue-eyed girl became fifteen instead of thirteen.

All her documents, even today, list 1924 as the year of her birth.

—

The German occupation also brought out the anti-Semitism of their neighbors. One Polish man began stealing from Jews since that was what the Germans themselves were doing. The Germans, however, did not appreciate the competition—the man was caught and put in jail. "He jumped from the third floor [of the jail] and killed himself."

Under Nazi policy, those who didn't work, didn't eat. The Leventals—Mottel and Bracha, and the three daughters who were still with them, Pola, Frimka, and Miriam—had no money and no work.

A neighbor—a man with five young children—started making soap out of margarine and oil. But he was afraid to sell it since Jews were banned from the marketplace and selling to or buying from non-Jews could mean death. In one case, a Jewish woman bought an egg for her starving child. Both she and the Pole who sold it were hanged, their bodies left in public view for a few days as a lesson to others.[22]

"I said to my mom, 'You know what, I can go to sell so I can make money for the family to eat.' So I was selling soap . . . outside the market, going around selling to the people. Even Germans, they were buying from me."

Although Miriam was wearing a Star of David, she spoke both German and Polish. "I was making money."

Her luck finally ran out. "Once I was holding one piece of soap in my hand and a German was after me, and he caught me. When he caught me, he opened up the paper and he wants to know who makes the soap. I say, 'I don't know. I bought it here in the market.' [He asks,] 'From who?' [I say,] 'I don't know.' He started to beat me to make me tell who made the soap. I say, 'I don't know. I don't know. I bought it. That's it. I don't know.'

"So he took me to the police and the police start to beat me to tell. I don't talk." The police sent Miriam to the Gestapo. In their attempt to get her to talk, the Gestapo turned a German shepherd on her. The dog tore her clothes and bit her, leaving scars she still carries with her.

When she still refused to reveal what she knew, she was sent to jail in a town a few hours away by train. The petite teen was locked up with prostitutes. Her plight elicited the sympathy of a German who was working in the jail.

"The German was there in the store sending vegetables [to Germans]." He asked Miriam if she could use a scale to put together the packages. "I always said I can do everything." So she got out of the jail cell and started putting together packages containing such things as carrots, potatoes, and onions.

She gave the completed packages to a Jewish boy who delivered them. "I said in Jewish [Yiddish] to the boy, 'I'm from Sosnowiec' and he's from Bedzin." She wrote down her name and address and gave him a letter for her parents, who didn't know where she was. After they received the letter, her mother used gold and diamond earrings to bribe Germans to let her out of jail.

Miriam was released one early evening in a strange town. "I was standing outside [the jail] looking which way to go to the train." A German was standing near her, so she asked him the way to the train. "He showed this," crossing his arms with fingers pointing in opposite directions.

The girl looked around. "On one side is light and the other side is no light. So I walked where the light is coming from. I walked and walked until I came to a building," which had light showing from the windows. It was getting dark and she was in danger of violating the curfew—and either going back to jail or being shot.

"I am standing and listening while someone talks, and I hear singing in Jewish and Polish, and the sewing machine was going. So I start to knock on the gate and to scream in Jewish, 'Please open the door for me!' [A man] came and looked out and saw me: 'What do you want here? It's already night coming and you are not allowed to be on the street.' I say, 'I know that. Please let me in. I am Jewish. I came out of jail. Please let me in.' They took me in."

Miriam had stumbled across a shop where a group of Jewish men and women were making German army uniforms. She told them what had happened to her and they fed her. Since she was not supposed to be there, her fellow Jews made a circle of some unfinished uniforms and put her in the middle, covering her up. If the Germans found her, she would be sent back to jail.

In the morning, Germans came to pick up finished uniforms and left without seeing her. After they were gone, the Jews in the shop gave her something to eat and put her on the train to Sosnowiec. When she arrived, she found her parents waiting for her at the station.

While Miriam was going through this, conditions in her hometown grew progressively worse in early 1941. Jews "were not allowed to go on the train" which ran through the middle of the ghetto, nor were Jews allowed on the main street.

Soon after she returned home, her father faced forced labor. "I heard the Germans coming. They are asking for our name. 'Where is Levental?' I heard Levental. I took my father and pushed him into a closet. And they came in: 'Where is your father?' I said, 'He is working.' [The German said,] 'What work is he doing?' I said, 'He is cleaning streets.'"

With Miriam's father in the closet and her mother not home, the girl told the Germans to take her instead.

And they did. "I took the key for the house and I said I have to give the key to the neighbor" so her parents could get in when they came home.

While she was being taken for forced labor, Miriam ran into a neighbor, a Jewish policeman, who lived two buildings down from

Miriam, center, is with two of her friends, all dressed for Purim 1938. (Courtesy of Miriam Apfel.)

her family. "He said, 'You're too young.' I said, 'I'm young but I know how to do everything.' The German she was with asked the policeman if he knew her, and he said, 'Yes, she is my neighbor. Her parents are my neighbors.'

Despite what the policeman said, Miriam was taken.

"They took me to the Jewish school. [Which was being used as a collection point for forced laborers.] They were making 600 girls stand in the school's backyard. They were making a group from this camp, this camp, this camp, and I heard them say 'This group goes to Markstadt,' where my brother was. I was not part of that group, so I said to the Jewish policemen who was taking care of my group that I was going to Markstadt because my brother is there. So he says, 'You have guts to talk to the German to change you?' I say, 'Yes.'" It took courage because Germans had shot Jews who asked to switch destinations. But in this case, a German was going around to the girls asking if they were happy about where they were going to work. "I say, 'Yes, I am very happy. I just want to beg that I want to go to Markstadt.' So he said to me, 'You are young and dumb. Here you can come home after work because it is close to your town.' I said, 'I don't care. I want to go to Markstadt because my brother is there.'"

The German switched Miriam with a girl in the group going to Markstadt. "They took us to the train and my mother was standing on the corner with two bottles of wine," one cherry and one blueberry. But the German guarding the girls would not let Bracha give her daughter the wine.

"So she said, 'You take one bottle and one bottle you give to my daughter." The German kept the cherry wine and gave the blueberry to Miriam. Bracha wanted her daughter to use the blueberry wine "when you have a pain in your belly, when you are not feeling good." Miriam would hold onto that wine, sipping it when she needed to and sharing it with Mylech.

On February 25, 1942, 100 Jewish men and 29 Jewish women were sent to Markstadt from Sosnowiec.[23]

Markstadt was built next to a Krupp armaments factory, Bertha-Werk, so the Jews could be used to produce weapons for the German army. The camp was about fourteen miles southeast of what was then Breslau, Germany, and today is Wroclaw, Poland. It was one of the largest of the Organization Schmelt forced labor camps. Operating from 1940 to 1944, the organization was named after its director, SS-Oberführer Albrecht Schmelt, who built forced-labor camps next to factories producing material for the army.[24] At its height in early 1943, the organization had 160 labor camps employing more than 50,000 Jewish forced laborers. Later in 1943, many of the camps were closed and the workers sent to Auschwitz. A few camps, such as Markstadt, were kept open because they were producing arms and munitions. The Organization Schmelt was dissolved in 1944 and the remaining camps were made part of Auschwitz, Gross-Rosen, and Blechhammer concentration camps.[25]

The Markstadt camp had about eighteen buildings surrounded by barbed wire. The barracks were built around a roll-call square, where prisoners were counted before and after work. Each barrack contained five rooms supervised by a *kapo*—a Jewish prisoner put in charge of other Jews and given special privileges. Each room could hold 26 to 40 people with bunk beds and one blanket for each straw mattress. The prisoners wore civilian clothing with Stars of David on their chests, backs, and pants.[26]

The forced laborers were woken before dawn and had to muster in the square to be counted, guarded by Germans with dogs. Anyone who was late was beaten by a kapo with a steel wire whip. At the camp gate, the prisoners were again counted and searched. One inmate, caught with a piece of bread, was savagely beaten. After work, the prisoners were marched back to camp where they were fed, after waiting for hours for their food, and counted again. Lights out was at 10 P.M.[27]

The Jews' daily rations consisted of a bowl of thin soup and one slice of bread. Spinach used in the soup was not washed, tasted bitter, and had stones. Turnips that normally were used for cattle feed were occasionally added to the soup. Many Jews starved to death. Some Jews who stole potatoes in an attempt to survive were caught and hanged. And it was not just the German guards who attacked the Jewish workers. Krupp's foremen and subcontractors also were violent. One inmate came back from work with his brains showing through his skull.[28]

This is the world Miriam entered.

"I am standing [in the camp], and walking by, I saw my brother's friend, and I called to him and I say, 'Where is my brother?' And he said, 'Stay by the kitchen, stay here, when the groups come from work your brother will be there.'"

The reunion was not what she expected. A man came up to her, claiming to be her brother. "I don't recognize him . . . I pushed him away. He said, 'I am your brother.' I pushed him away, 'You're not my brother.' He started to cry . . . he started to talk. I recognized his voice. He was like a skeleton; he was a big man. After he started to talk to me, and say the name of my mother, my father, my sisters, I recognize him." Their reunion ended when Mylech had to go get food and then return to the barracks.

Miriam was put to work washing clothes. That consisted of using a metal scrubbing board in a tub. As she worked, blood began running from her fingers. She had scrubbed the clothes so hard that she had injured her fingers. "I went out and I was standing, letting the blood surround me. A man went by in a

Yehuda Apfel, 1941, while he was a member of the Jewish Brigade with the British Army. (Courtesy of Miriam Apfel.)

shiny car and he looked at me. He said, 'What happened to you?' And I said, 'I can't wash clothes. I never have washed clothes.'"

She was taken to a doctor who bandaged her hands. "The doctor says, 'What can you do?' I say, 'Anything but washing clothes.'"

So Miriam was sent to peel potatoes. She had to fill a barrel with peeled potatoes each day. The problem was that the barrel was too large for her to be able to do that.

A German asked what the petite blue-eyed, blond girl who spoke good German could do for work. "I say, 'Everything but not peel potatoes.' So he looked at me: 'Do you know how to work on a scale?' I say, 'Yes.'" Miriam didn't know if she could but thought it was worth a try. She was taken to where produce was packaged for Germans. She watched another worker using a scale and making a package. For the next two years, she was packaging potatoes, sugar, flour, and rice. And she ate some herself and filled her pockets to smuggle food to her brother.

Mylech was working with a crew building a railroad. Miriam would smuggle food to him, and he would share it with the other Jews. They cooked potatoes over a fire they had to keep warm, being careful not to let the Germans guarding them notice what they were doing.

"I had bread and all kinds of stuff and gave it to my brother. And my brother was with fifteen boys, men, in a room, and he divided it up and gave each one a piece of Hanukkah."

That ended because of another Jew's jealousy. In late December 1943, the German who liked her gave Miriam two apples.

An older Jew where Miriam worked told her, "'Your brother is having food like a pig already. You deliver it.' I said, 'Yes, I am giving him my soup and I am eating in the kitchen.' . . . He was jealous that I brought the apples to my brother and not to him." In retribution, he put her to work somewhere else—away from the food.

When the German who liked her found out, he put her to work in the kitchen where food was prepared for the Jewish forced workers.

Miriam worked in there until the camp was closed March 25, 1944.[29]

The men and women were sent to different camps. Miriam went to Peterswaldau Concentration Camp in Lower Silesia, one of the 77 subcamps of the Gross-Rosen Concentration Camp.[30] She was put to work making munitions for the Wehrmacht.

During a shift, a Polish woman caught her hand in a machine and began screaming. As Miriam bent down to turn off the equipment and help the woman, her hair was caught in the machinery, which ripped out not only hair but also some of her scalp on the right side of her head, leaving a scar she bears to this day. The Pole lost two fingers and Miriam had a bleeding head.

A group of Hungarian Jews had just arrived. They wore scarves, so Miriam put a scarf on and blended in with them, fearful that if the Germans discovered she was bleeding she would be sent to Auschwitz.

The two camp doctors—one, a Russian doctor who had smuggled herself in from Auschwitz with the Hungarian Jews—hid Miriam and the woman she had helped. Ultimately, the Pole went to work in the kitchen.

While Miriam was in the hospital, "my parents came to me in a dream . . . and said to me, 'Miriam, this is not a place for you. This is a dangerous place. Go to work.' . . . In the morning, I woke up, I was like sweating. I went out of the hospital and the doctor and the nurse are standing there. They say, 'Where are you going?' . . . [I said,] 'I'm going to work.' They say, 'You have a fever. How can you go to work?' And I said, 'I have to go because my mother, my father came to me and said not to be here . . . just go to work. I listen to them.'"

With the help of three others—"A girl was pushing me and two girls were holding me"—Miriam went to work in the kitchen that day.

When she returned to the hospital that evening, all the patients were gone. About fifteen women had been in the hospital with her that morning. The Germans sent them all to be gassed at Auschwitz.

Miriam and the other forced laborers were liberated May 8, 1945, by the Soviet Red Army, a day after the official German surrender. "That was my best birthday present," even if it was two days late.

Freedom started with a peek through a window.

Miriam and the other women had been locked inside their barracks, each room furnished with three-tier bunk beds with blankets over the windows to block the view outside. "We couldn't even go to the bathroom."

When they heard a commotion outside, Miriam, who was on the top bunk, wanted to see what was going on—so she pulled the blanket back. "The girls start to scream, 'What are you doing? You are going to kill us!'" What Miriam saw was the German soldiers releasing the cows and chickens from their pens and leaving. "I say, 'Something is happening! Something is happening!'"

Suddenly, a Czechoslovakian came and started to scream, "Girls, this is the liberation! We are free!"

Czechs, who were living outside the camp, had been working for the Germans. After the soldiers left, the Czechs opened the camp's gates.

Yehuda Apfel, 1944, while he was a member of the Jewish Brigade with the British Army. (Courtesy of Miriam Apfel.)

The fleeing German soldiers cut the buttons off their uniforms and shed as much of their uniforms as they could to avoid being picked up by Red Army soldiers.

Liberation came too late for most of the Jews left in Sosnowiec, including her parents and one of her sisters. They had been sent to the extermination camp in Auschwitz-Birkenau. The deportations started in August 1940 with those who had committed some offense but had not been killed on the spot.[31]

Then, in early 1941, the Jews were ordered to move into Szrodula, a suburb of Sosnowiec, where a ghetto was established. A transit camp was set up to send Jews who did not have permanent jobs to forced labor camps. Starting in March 1942, groups of sixty to seventy Jews were sent each week to their deaths in Auschwitz, about 24 miles to the south. These were usually Jews who had broken the rules, such as not wearing a Star of David or violating curfew, as well as Jews suspected of political activity.[32]

The first large scale deportation happened in May 1942 when 1,500 old and sick Jews from Sosnowiec and Bedzin were sent to their deaths in Auschwitz, despite promises that they would not be harmed.[33]

In June, German soldiers invaded the Jewish hospital, taking women who had just given birth, people who had had surgery, and all the babies from the children's ward. The babies were thrown from the second floor into trucks waiting on the street. All were sent to their deaths in Auschwitz.[34]

While small numbers of Jews were often sent to Auschwitz or forced labor camps, the next major deportation did not take place until August 12, 1942, when all the Jews were ordered to assemble in the ghetto square. They were surrounded by SS troops and German police. In a selection that lasted until midnight, each Jew was put into one of four categories:[35]

- Those who worked in factories the German war effort needed. They were allowed to return to their homes.
- Those who were to be sent to forced labor camps.
- Those who were marked for death.
- Those whose fate had not been decided.[36]

Anyone who tried to move from one group to another was killed.[37]

All those in the last three groups were kept in the square until the next morning when the approximately 12,000 whose fate had been decided were held in designated buildings. The first transport left on August 13, taking about 2,000 Jews to die in Auschwitz. Ten days later, about 6,000 were sent to the Birkenau gas chambers at Auschwitz, while 2,000 to 3,000 were sent to forced labor camps. In February 1943, another several thousand Jews were sent to forced labor camps.[38]

In June 1943, the Germans launched a large-scale action, but most of the Jews succeeded in hiding, so only about 1,000 were sent to Auschwitz. During July, the Germans did not attempt to raid the ghetto and most Jews no longer went to work, having discovered that offered no protection.[39]

Members of the Jewish youth organization managed to form an underground movement and got weapons. Sentries were posted to warn the residents of any new moves by the Germans, who published notices calling on able-bodied Jews to volunteer to work in Germany. Few responded.[40]

In mid-June, the head of the local SS invited Merin and four of his council members to a meeting. They were never seen again.[41]

The Germans launched a large-scale action on August 1, 1943—a Sunday. That surprised the Jews because it was the first time the Germans had attacked on a Sunday.[42]

The Germans surrounded the ghetto at 2 A.M. and launched an attack which lasted four days. The Jewish underground fought back but was quickly defeated by the better-armed, more-numerous Germans.[43]

During the search of every house, about 1,000 men, women, and children were killed. When a bunker was discovered, soldiers would first fire into it and then throw in grenades to ensure that everyone would die. Children who had lost their parents were either put into sacks and thrown onto trucks or killed by soldiers who beat their heads on the sidewalks. Between 30,000 and 35,000 were sent to Birkenau, packed 120 to 150 into train cattle cars. Many suffocated on the trip.[44]

Despite the Nazis' efforts, not all the Jews had been found. So, on August 3, 1943, German authorities announced that the remaining Jews could leave their hideouts for a special camp where they would be allowed to stay. About 2,000 Jews responded to the offer. A few days later, several hundred were sent to Auschwitz.[45]

When the action ended, 150 Jews were kept in the ghetto to collect the property of those who had been deported or killed. Another 300 were working in tailoring shops. In September and October, those 300 were sent to labor camps in Upper Silesia. And occasionally, the Gestapo would send Jews from the special camp to Auschwitz. By December 1943, some 400 Jews were left in Sosnowiec.[46]

—

On May 8, 1945, all Miriam knew was that she was free and still alive.

This card with a photo of Miriam and Yehuda Apfel with their new daughter, Bracha, was made for their first Rosh Hashanah in Israel. (Courtesy of Miriam Apfel.)

Soviet soldiers arrived soon after the Czechs opened the camp. The Red Army troops told the survivors, "Go, live in the Germans' houses." The German civilians had fled from the triumphant Red Army.

"I was walking on the street, all of a sudden came three bicycles and three boys, and I recognized a cousin." Miriam was in such shock she couldn't speak. All she could do was to gesture at them.

Her cousin, Hunek Steinfeld, realized who she was, and "he started to scream, 'This is my cousin! This is my cousin!' And I start to cry and I start to talk."

Her cousin was living in a German's apartment with three other boys, a situation Miriam found uncomfortable. Hunek told her to bring another girl with her. "I took another friend and went to live with him." Her cousin soon left for Czechoslovakia after he had learned his sister was there, having survived the Holocaust.

After a bit, the other boys in the apartment decided to return to Sosnowiec. Miriam wanted to go as well to look for members of her family. "They didn't want to take me because the soldiers, the Russians, were looking for girls to rape." But she insisted, and the boys finally relented. As a precaution, she took a blanket covered in coal dust. When they stopped to rest, the boys covered her with it. "The Russians came around looking for girls and said, 'If you find girls send them to us.'" She was never discovered.

When she reached Sosnowiec—about 126 miles southeast of the camp she had been in—she first found her brother's wife, Tsesha, in an apartment cooking for concentration camp survivors. Mylech was missing. Tesha had survived Auschwitz, but her three-year-old child had been murdered.

"She never got over that. She was a nice woman."

Miriam moved in with Tsesha and began looking for her brother. She would go to the train station because the Red Cross was bringing sick people back. "One came screaming from the train, 'Miriam, your brother, he's alive!'" When she was told where he was, "I said, 'I am going to Theresienstadt to my brother to look for him.'"

But her brother's friend told her to wait because Mylech was in the hospital and the Red Cross would be bringing him to Sosnowiec on another train from Theresienstadt Concentration Camp, more than 329 miles to the west. Mylech was among the approximately 17,000 Jews who were still alive when the camp in Czechoslovakia was liberated by the Red Army. More than 154,000 Jews had been sent to Theresienstadt during the war. Of those, more than half, 88,000, were sent to extermination camps, while another 33,000 died of starvation or the brutal treatment at the hands of the Germans and their collaborators.[47]

"I was standing by the train waiting for another transport and my brother came. They took him to a . . . Jewish hospital in our town. . . . They took all the sick people from the camps to the hospital."

Miriam then went back to Tsesha and suggested they visit the hospital to see if they could find anyone they knew. "I didn't want to tell her her husband was alive because he was a skeleton, skin and bones. . . . She went with me and I hid his name on the bed. He recognized her and started to scream, 'Tsesha, I am your husband!' Both started to scream and cry, and I was crying."

Mylech was in the hospital for two weeks, and then Miriam took him and Tsesha to Peterswaldau "where I was in the camp because over there were farms from the Germans." Czechs and Poles were working on the farms and gave them food, including butter, milk, and cheese. "We start to eat like human beings and we got weight on, and we went back to Sosnowiec."

Her three sisters, Regina, Adeaa, and Nadia; Regina's husband, Moshe; and her children, Asher, who has now nine years old, and Leah, who was six, returned after spending the war in the Soviet Union, having managed to stay ahead of the German advance. Her sister, Frimka, returned from Auschwitz. Her parents and sister, Pola, were murdered there.

By August 1945, the surviving members of the family had left Poland, ending up in western Germany, which had been occupied by the Americans, British, and French.

"In Poland there was anti-Semitism. They look on us like garbage." The Poles told the Jews, "There is no room for you. Go to Palestine." The Poles thought the Germans had killed all the Jews. "But we came home. We knocked on the door and I saw everything bought by our parents." The Poles told Miriam that when the Germans took her parents away, they had bought everything from the Leventals.

"What can you do?"

Poland after the war was not a safe place for Jews because of the anti-Semitism. Anti-Jewish riots broke out in Krakow on August 20, followed by riots in Sosnowiec on October 25 and Lublin on November 19. Seven months after the war had ended, 350 Jews had been murdered by Poles, including four delegates who were killed on a train from Lodz while they were on their way to a Jewish communal convention.

Jews again faced ritual murder accusations in Krakow and Rzeszow, and a hospital for Jewish orphans was attacked in Radom. Two Jews who were injured in an attack on a bus in Lublin were then tracked to the hospital they were in and murdered in their beds. Also in Lublin, Chaim Hirszman, one of the two survivors of the Belzec Extermination Camp, was murdered on his way home from his first day of testimony about what happened there. He was killed because he was a Jew.[48]

Mylech and his wife went to Munich, in Bavaria in southern Germany. Miriam and Frimka had gone to Austria from Poland and now planned to join Mylech in Munich, which was in the American Zone of Occupation. Germany had been divided into four occupation zones with the Americans in the south, British in the northwest, French in the southwest, and Soviets in the east. Berlin was also split into four occupation zones. West Germany, formally the Federal Republic of Germany, was formed in May 1949 out of the three western occupation zones, and the western allies formally ended their occupation in 1955. East Germany, formally the German Democratic Republic, was created in 1949 out of the Soviet zone. The two Germanies were reunited in 1990 after the collapse of the Soviet Union.[49]

Reaching Munich proved challenging for Miriam and Frimka. "We were on the train going from Austria to Munich," but they didn't have any money so they didn't have tickets. The official checking tickets tried to get them off the train at a stop. As the train started to move again, Frimka was still onboard. The nineteen-year-old petite Miriam pushed the official down and hopped back on, riding all the way to Munich.

Miriam and her family members went to Munich because there was a Jewish community of concentration camp survivors and others who were looking for their family members. Miriam and her sister and brother were looking for cousins. "We didn't find anybody."

Despite the occupation, Jews still faced problems in Munich. When Miriam, Mylech, and the others went to get an apartment, the German landlady would not let them in "because she was a Nazi." Mylech appealed to the German police for help, who forced the woman out of that apartment and into the basement. "They gave us an apartment, a beautiful apartment . . . three rooms, a kitchen, a dining room and a bathroom with a bathtub and everything." They got food with coupons issued to them by the Germans. Mylech's daughter, Sarah, was born in Munich.

After a month in Munich, Miriam and Frimka moved to the Displaced Persons Camp in Deggendorf, Germany, about nintey miles to the northwest. "We found our oldest sister and her husband in Deggendorf. . . . They were living in a camp for the [American] Army and everyone had a room and was getting food from the Americans."

Between 1945 and 1952 more than 250,000 Jews lived in DP camps, administered by the United Nations Relief and Rehabilitation Administration, in and around cities in Germany, Austria, and Italy. They were among the approximately 11 million refugees set adrift in the aftermath of World War II. About seven million were in the western areas occupied by the Allies, including both Jewish and non-Jewish concentration camp survivors and slave laborers, former prisoners of war from various nations, and people who fled in the face of the fighting and had lost their homes.

—

The Allies originally planned to return refugees to their homelands, but that wouldn't work for Jews who faced vicious anti-Semitism in eastern Europe. Having few options, Palestine became the destination of choice for many—a place where they could have some control over their destinies in a Jewish society. Zionists, including agents sent from British-controlled Palestine, and members of the British army's Jewish Brigade worked to recruit Jews. *Kibbutzim* were set up to teach agricultural skills to the prospective immigrants.[50]

Standing in the way were the British, who, despite promises to create a Jewish homeland made in the Balfour Declaration issued during World War I, were doing all they could to block Jews from immigrating in an effort to appease Arabs.[51]

Britain had gained control of Palestine—present-day Israel, the West Bank, and Jordan—after the breakup of the Turkish Empire following its defeat in World War I, under a mandate from the League of Nations, the failed forerunner of the United Nations.[52]

Restrictions on Jewish immigration began in 1922 and became tougher as World War II approached, with a ceiling of 1,500 per month. After the war, the Royal Navy established a blockade of the Palestinian coast, taking most of their Jewish captives to Cyprus where they were locked behind barbed wire until the British evacuated Palestine in 1948. Britain also pressured European countries, such as Italy, Greece, and France, to keep Jews from using their territories as routes to Palestine. And the British sought to stop the Jewish purchase of ships used to smuggle immigrants across the Mediterranean Sea.[53]

When Miriam and Frimka reached Deggendorf, finding the DP camp where their sister Regina was proved challenging. Not only did they not know where the camp was, they didn't know about the curfew that was in force.

"There was a German on the train, too, who knew . . . to run home. I and my sister didn't know where to go." Then, American soldiers caught all three of them and started to beat not only the German, but Miriam and Frimka as well. The Americans thought all three were Germans. Part of the problem was that they "didn't look Jewish." Both had light hair and blue eyes. "My sister took to show [the number tattooed on her arm in Auschwitz] we are not German, we are Jews from concentration camps. . . . And they took us to the police station.

Yehuda and Miriam Apfel, 1993. (Courtesy of Miriam Apfel.)

"I said to the police, 'Who speak German? Who speak Polish? Who speak Jewish [Yiddish]?' So one came and said, 'I speak Jewish.' So he start to talk to us . . . and ask who we are and my sister showed him the number [on her arm from Auschwitz]."

With that proof, the soldiers took the two to the DP Camp, where they started looking for Regina and her family. Finally, they found her—Regina, her husband, and their two children were living in one room. So Miriam stayed with one neighbor, while Frimka was with another. The next day, the two sisters were given their own place.

One day Miriam and Frimka had gone to a movie when Miriam became ill. "I had a terrible pain in my stomach. . . . I went back to the camp and my sister (Regina) was not home," having gone to the kibbutz to celebrate the Sabbath. The two young women were standing outside their sister's door when neighbors came out and asked them what was wrong. Frimka told them Miriam was in pain, so they took her to the camp's hospital where she was given medicine. When they returned, Regina had not returned home, so Miriam sat in front of the locked door.

A neighbor opened the door and said, "You can't sit outside." Not feeling well, Miriam went in and sat on a bed.

"All of a sudden two soldiers came in." One was wearing a Polish uniform and the other a British; both were Jews and both were working with *Haganah*, the Jewish self-defense force which had been organized after Arabs began attacking Jews in Palestine and the British did little to interfere.

"I was ashamed" to be seen in the state she was in, so Miriam decided to see if her sister had come home. "The British soldier said, 'I am going with you. I don't want you to go alone.'"

Miriam didn't know the people who took her in or the soldier who went with her. The soldier was Judah Apfel, the man she would someday marry. The couple who took her in would become her father- and mother-in-law. Judah's parents, Moshe and Ella Apfel, had survived the war by fleeing to the Soviet Union from Krakow when the Germans invaded.

Judah spent the war fighting the Germans. Born in 1926, he had run away from home and enlisted in the Polish army when he was thirteen years old, just before the German invasion. He was big for his age and claimed to be seventeen. After Poland's defeat in September 1939, thousands of Polish soldiers managed to escape to join the French and British in their war against Germany. Some, such as Judah, went to Palestine. There he connected with the *Haganah*, and like other Palestinian Jews, he enlisted in the Jewish Brigade which had been formed by the British army. The Brigade ended the war fighting in Italy with the British 8th Army.

After the war, Judah went searching for his parents, finding them in Krakow. By 1946, he had moved them to the Displaced Persons Camp in Deggendorf. That is where he met Miriam, sitting on a bed not feeling well. The couple married on February 8, 1947, in Deggendorf, and would eventually make it to Israel. Judah's parents also reached Israel. Miriam's surviving siblings either stayed in Western Europe or emigrated to the United States and Canada.

Miriam and Judah were determined to immigrate to Palestine, despite the British blockade. Judah was a member of a group which bought a ship from a Greek owner. The *Theodor Herzl* set sail, flying the Israeli flag, for Palestine from Sete on the French

Mediterranean coast, on April 2, 1947, with 2,641 passengers on board.[54]

The freighter reached Haifa, but most of the passengers did not reach the shore. Two British destroyers came along both sides of the *Herzl*, squeezing the ship and allowing soldiers to board. Fighting broke out as the British sought to gain control. "We were throwing cans of food at them. Just throwing things at them." During the melee, the British opened fire, killing three Jews and wounding more. After putting down the uprising, the British took the wounded and sick to the Atlit detention camp, which was 12.5 miles south of Haifa, established to keep Jews out of Palestine.[55]

Miriam and Judah Apfel, along with the rest of the passengers, were interned in prison camps on Cyprus, an island some 293 miles northwest of Palestine. Their first child, a daughter named Bracha, after the mother Miriam lost in the Holocaust, was born June 5, 1948, behind the camp's barbed wire. The internees were kept imprisoned until the British left Palestine and Israel declared its independence on May 14, 1948.

But they were not able to reach Israel until after the War of Independence had ended with armistice agreements signed with the surrounding Arab nations, first with Egypt on February 24, 1949, and finally with Syria on July 20. The Israelis used ships the British had seized, including the *Herzl*, to bring the Jews from Cyprus.

The Apfels were among the last survivors to come from Cyprus, arriving on the last ship.

In 1948, Israel was a poor country that had just fought a war and was dealing with the influx of hundreds of thousands of Jews from Europe, followed soon after by about 750,000 Jews who were forced out of Arab countries where their ancestors had been living for 1,000 years or more.

Living conditions were primitive.

"I was in a [tent] camp in Israel. Then we got an apartment. We had a roof . . . no [running] water, no toilet. I had to go down from the second floor to the backyard to the toilet, to wash. One toilet in the backyard for ten people, and a shower, a spigot for water. When it was raining, I put the raincoat on my daughter's bed [because] the rain was coming in. I had water coming from the ceiling."

Their apartment was built in a vacant building that had been used for business in the town of Netyana on the Mediterranean coast about twenty miles north of Tel Aviv. "I was paying five dollars a month [in rent] and my husband was in the army." He later joined the police force as an undercover officer. Their son was born July 28, 1952, in Israel.

One day in 1958, Miriam and Judah went to see a movie, *Gone with the Wind.* Their fourteen-year-old daughter, Bracha, was home watching her brother. One of the rules when her parents were not home: Don't open the door.

While they were gone, a man and woman from the United States knocked on the apartment door.

At first, Bracha refused to open the door. "They said to me, 'We don't know if we have the right people. Her name used to be Miriam Levental. . . . We don't know what your name is now. She used to be a little girl, with blond hair, four foot five or six, she had five sisters and a brother. The name was Levental.' So I said, 'Yeah, that's my mother.'" The man was one of the boys Miriam had helped to survive in Markstadt Concentration Camp.

Bracha opened the door to Henry and Uba Weinroth.

She asked a neighbor to watch her brother as she went to get her parents. Bracha ran downtown to the movie theater. "We knew the usher. Everybody knew everybody in those days, and I said, 'Go tell my *aba* [father] and *ema* [mother] that some people from America are looking for them because she saved the man's life.'"

The three of them rode home on the family's bicycle: Miriam on the front, Judah peddling, and Bracha on the rear.

When they opened the door to their third-floor apartment, they looked at each other—and then all five of them started crying and yelling and laughing. Henry told Miriam, "You never grew up. You stayed small." Meanwhile, Miriam's six-year-old son, Marty, was standing there, wondering what was going on.

What was going on was that eight of the boys Miriam had helped to survive had emigrated to the United States and were all living in Stamford, Connecticut. When they learned Miriam was living in Israel, they pooled their money and sent Henry and his wife in search of her. They wanted to thank her for saving their lives and to invite her to move to Stamford. Judah agreed to leave Israel after his uncle, who had immigrated to the United States well before the war, promised him a good job with his furniture company in the Bronx in New York City.

It took the Apfels six years to get the visas they needed to immigrate. The job Judah was to have was working in the company's

Miriam celebrating Simcha Torah—the Joy of the Torah—in 2016. (Courtesy of Miriam Apfel.)

office. They were also told Stamford was an eight-hour trip from the Bronx. Neither proved to be true.

Miriam didn't care for the Bronx—there were no trees, no flowers, just buildings. But she had "a beautiful apartment. I have furniture already."

A few months after arriving, she got a call from a cousin. "She saw [Judah] schlepping [moving] furniture on his back. She called me, 'Miriam, what is doing with your husband?' I said, 'He is working by his uncle in the office.' So she said, 'Miriam, are you sitting or standing?' I said, 'I'm standing by the telephone.' [She said,] 'Sit down.' I say, 'I'm sitting.' 'Your husband is not working in the office. He is schlepping furniture from the fourth floor. No elevator.'"

Miriam called the office and said she needed her husband to come home immediately to help with their children's English for school. "I said, 'He is not coming to work. Today is his last day. I don't let him go anymore to work.'"

She called their friends in Stamford—and found out it was only one hour away. Their friends found an apartment for them. A week later, Henry and others came to the Bronx with a truck and they moved to Stamford. Judah began working as a plumber with another friend. "He was a handyman—went from being a cop to a plumber."

Miriam and Judah lived in Stamford for fifteen years. Bracha was married by then and Judah had heart problems. The couple moved to Montreal to be near relatives and friends, but Canada's winters proved too much for Judah. So after two years, they moved to Los Angeles, near other relatives and friends. Judah died in April 1993. In 1994, Miriam moved to Florida to be near her daughter.

Miriam survived the Holocaust because she never gave up, never stopped trying to survive, or helping others to survive even at the risk of her own life.

"I believe in God always. I wake up [in the concentration camp], I see a tin cup with ice in it and I am going to work and I am alive. I believe I have to make a purpose. I believe always I have to be alive and see the family. I say, 'God help me.' I was praying every day to be alive."

NOTES

1. www.edwarvictor.com.
2. Centenary News, https://centenarynews.com.
3. Centenary News.
4. Culture.pl.
5. Culture.pl.
6. Leni Yahil, *The Holocaust: The Fate of European Jewry* (n.p.: Oxford University Press, 1987): 207.
7. Virtual Shtetl Museum of Polish Jews Polin, sztetl.org.pl.
8. www.jewishgen.org, *The Destruction of Kozinece—Holocaust*, 436.
9. William L. Shirer, *The Rise and Fall of the Third Reich* (n.p.: MLF Books, 1988): 439–541.
10. Shirer, *The Rise and Fall*, 634.
11. Shirer, *The Rise and Fall*, 633-634.
12. Shirer, *The Rise and Fall*, 626.
13. Holocaust Education & Archive Research Team, www.holocaustresearchproject.org.
14. Holocaust Matters, www.holocaustmatters.org.
15. Gerald Reitlinger, *The Final Solution: The Attempt to Exterminate the Jews 1939–1945* (n.p.: Jason Aronson Inc., 1987): 37.
16. Reitlinger, *The Final Solution: The Attempt*, 285.
17. Yahil, *The Holocaust: The Fate*, 207.
18. Yahil, *The Holocaust: The Fate*, 207.
19. Martin Gilbert, *The Holocaust: A History of the Jews of Europe During the Second World War* (n.p.; Holt, Rinehart and Winston, 1985).
20. Yahil, *The Holocaust: The Fate*, 208.
21. Holocaust Education & Archive Research Team
22. Gilbert, *The Holocaust: A History*, 146.
23. Holocaust Matters.
24. Holocaust Matters.
25. Yad Vashem, https://www.yadvashem.org.
26. Holocaust Matters.
27. Holocaust Matters.
28. Holocaust Matters.
29. Holocaust Matters.
30. JewishGen, https://www.jewishgen.org.
31. Holocaust Education & Archive Research Team.
32. Holocaust Education & Archive Research Team.

33. Holocaust Education & Archive Research Team.
34. Gilbert, *The Holocaust: A History*, 365.
35. Holocaust Education & Archive Research Team.
36. Holocaust Education & Archive Research Team.
37. Holocaust Education & Archive Research Team.
38. Holocaust Education & Archive Research Team.
39. Holocaust Education & Archive Research Team.
40. Holocaust Education & Archive Research Team.
41. Gilbert, *The Holocaust: A History*, 585.
42. Holocaust Education & Archive Research Team.
43. Holocaust Education & Archive Research Team.
44. Holocaust Education & Archive Research Team.
45. Holocaust Education & Archive Research Team.
46. Holocaust Education & Archive Research Team.
47. Jewish Virtual Library, https://www.jewishvirtuallibrary.org.
48. Gilbert, *The Holocaust: A History*, 816-817.
49. History, www.history.com.
50. Holocaust Encyclopedia.
51. Aliya Bet (Ha'apala), www.palyam.org.
52. Aliya Bet (Ha'apala).
53. Aliya Bet (Ha'apala).
54. Aliya Bet (Ha'apala).
55. Aliya Bet (Ha'apala).

"Why would God help me and not help six million people . . . I couldn't believe it."

—Rene Hammond

CHAPTER 3

TWO SISTERS

Rene Hammond, formerly Rene Konigsberg

Rene Hammond at 93 years old is a widow, a mother, a grandmother, and great-grandmother. As a teenager, she survived the Holocaust.

She was born Rene Konigsberg on December 25, 1925, in Uzhorod, Czechoslovakia, the middle of three children of Ferdinand and Theodora Konigsberg.

Her Orthodox Jewish parents were both born in 1898 in what was then the eastern part of the Austro-Hungarian Empire. Her brother, Adolf, was two years older. Her sister, Agnes, two years younger. Their father owned two furniture stores.

"We lived a sheltered life. Whatever we wanted, we could get, you know. . . . Our life was pretty normal, observing all the [Jewish] holidays and going to school and planning to go to college."

After the Austro-Hungary Empire was broken up following World War I, Uzhorod became part of the new nation of Czechoslovakia on September 10, 1919.[1]

Following the Munich Agreement, which gave the Czech Sudetenland to Germany, Uzhorod became part of Hungary, a German ally, in November 1938.[2]

"We spoke Hungarian," since the family was now in that country.

Jewish life took a turn for the worse under Hungarian rule. "We had a curfew, not being out late after a certain time. Then the law came in that we have to have a yellow star when we were out so they would recognize us."

And her father was forced to take on a non-Jewish partner in his business. "Jews couldn't have their own businesses. We used to have a maid in the house, non-Jewish; that was not allowed anymore."

Another change was that Jewish children could no longer attend Hungarian schools.

"Fortunately, there was a Hebrew gymnasium [high school] in town, so we could transfer." Ultimately, that proved to be a good move "because in the Hungarian school the foreign languages were French, German and Russian. In the Hebrew school, we learned English and Hebrew." For Rene and her sister, the three years of English "came in very handy after the war."

And under the new Hungarian laws, college was out of the question for Jews. "One of my cousins who was in medical school had to get out. He couldn't finish because he was Jewish."

World War II broke out on September 1, 1939, when Germany invaded Poland, and France and Britain declared war on Germany. Hungary was a German ally.

Rene was fifteen years old; her brother, Adolf, was seventeen; and Agnes was thirteen. Their parents were forty-two years old.

During the winter of 1939-40, Hungary ordered the expulsion of all Jews of Polish or Czech citizenship, shipping them in cattle cars to German-occupied Poland.

"My father found out that they were going to deport people. So at that point my family got on the train [for Budapest]. . . . In a big city like that, people don't know you so you could get lost. . . . We stayed there for a few weeks until he got word that . . . it was safe to go home."

In 1940 and 1941, the Hungarian government forced hundreds of Jews into labor battalions, and after June 1941, sent others to the Eastern Front to fight against the Soviet Union, where most of them died.[3] Then, in late July and early August 1941, dozens

A family photograph with parents, Theodora and Ferdinand Konigsberg, in front. Behind them, from right, is Rene, Adolf, and Agnes. (Courtesy of Rene Hammond.)

of Jewish families who did not hold Hungarian citizenship were expelled and murdered.[4]

By 1944, the Soviet Union had turned the tables on the Germans, driving the Nazis and their allies west.

In March 1944, Germany occupied its crumbling Hungarian ally, and on March 19, German troops entered Uzhorod.[5]

The Germans set up an improvised ghetto in the Moskovits brickyard on Minai Street. On Passover, April 21 to 23, 1944, the approximately 25,000 Jews in Uzhorod and the surrounding area were forced into the ghetto.[6] When the brickyard was full, the Germans opened a second ghetto at the Gluck lumberyard.[7]

"In '44, I remember we had the last Passover dinner. We were lucky because the Polish Jews were taken much sooner."

Before they were taken to the ghettos, the Jews were told "they would have to go and work on a farm in Hungary. We could take with us whatever we could carry, food and clothing."

In an attempt to save something, the family gave to her father's non-Jewish employees "a lot of things before we were taken away to hide it for us so when we came back we will have it. Of course, we never went back."

When the day came, "the Hungarian military came into the house and got us out, marched us down the street with people lined up watching us." The watchers were silent as the Jews passed by.

The ghetto "was walled in, you know you just couldn't go in and out of it." There were "tents for us with straw on the floor where we supposed to sleep."

Rene and her family, and the other Jews were held there for a few weeks.

While she was in the ghetto, "I had a [non-Jewish] girlfriend" who "brought me some food, handed it over the fence." Rene and Irene Turak had met when they attended the Hungarian school together.

"We stayed there a few weeks, and then they gathered us up and said, 'We're ready to take you to the farm.'"

From May 17 to 31, 1944, the ghettos were emptied as five trains of cattle cars carried the Jews to Auschwitz.[8] The Red Army did not reach the area until November. Only a few hundred from those transports are believed to have survived.

"They packed too many people into those railroad cars. All you could do is sit in one place. You could hardly get up, and that naturally, we couldn't lie down."

During the three days and three nights they were on the train, they did not know they were headed for Auschwitz Concentration Camp.

"They didn't give us anything" to eat or drink during the trip. "They just kept us in there. We could eat whatever we took with us."

It was night when they pulled into the yard at Auschwitz, detraining in the glare of big floodlights. They could see the flames from what they later learned was the crematorium.

First men were separated from women. Then, the older women and younger women with children were separated from the younger women without children.

"My mother was forty-six years old, but she was considered old."

The guards said the older women and women with children would be taken to get showers first, while the childless younger women would walk to the showers later.

"That sounded reasonable. Well, that's the last time I saw my father and the last time I saw my mother."

On the way to the showers, "I saw old bearded men lying in the gutters. I didn't know if they were dead; they must have been."

The younger women and men got showers, and had their heads shaved, "so we were completely bald."

Before showering, "they told us to put all our possessions, clothes and shoes and whatever we brought with us, into a neat little pile because, after the shower, you'll get them back."

But instead of getting their belongings, each woman received a prisoner's dress with numbers on it, along with wooden shoes and a blanket. No underwear.

"We weren't tattooed because we were supposed to be taken from Auschwitz to Germany and work in factories."

From the showers, Rene, her sister, and others were taken to barracks. The bunks, built one on top of the other, were "about as big as single bed."

"But each bed had six people on them," so the women could not lie down.

"We could just sit and wait. What will happen? We wondered. We were scared and clung to each other."

It was when they were in the barracks that they asked when they would see their parents.

The answer: "You'll never see your parents again. They're dead."

From other prisoners, Rene learned about the gas chambers masquerading as showers and the crematorium.

Her brother, Adolf, was assigned to work in the crematorium in what the Germans called a *Sonderkommando*, pulling the bodies of fellow Jews from the gas chambers and carting them to the crematorium.

"My brother could hardly ever talk about what he had to do."

Rene and her sister were in Auschwitz for about six weeks, waiting for their fate.

During periodic selections for slave labor in German factories, the women were forced to walk in circles. "I remember one of those selections where we had to walk in the nude to be picked."

Finally, Rene and Agnes were selected with about 500 other women to work in the German war industry.

After one factory where they were scheduled to work was destroyed in an Allied bombing raid, the women were taken to a Krupp steel factory in Essen, a major industrial city in the northern Ruhr, along the Rhine River in western Germany.

"Conditions were pretty miserable, because during the winter months, some of the girls had to carry these big metal sheets . . . [and] almost froze to the metal."

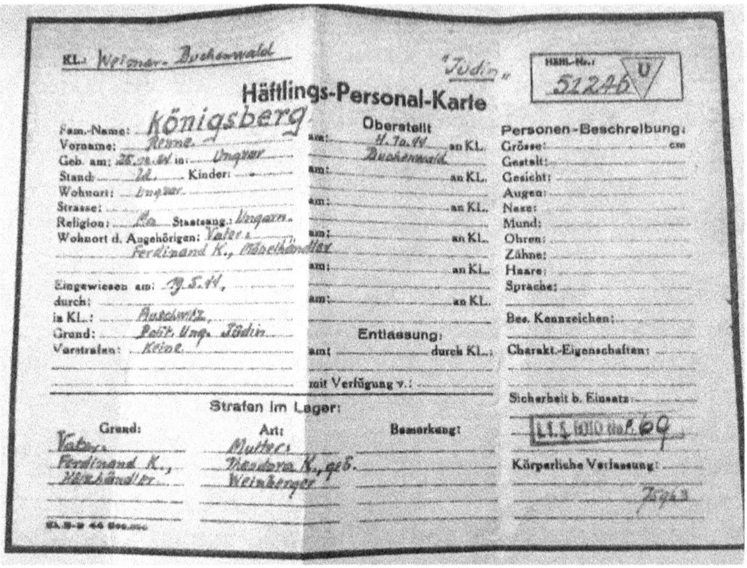

KL.: Weimar-Buchenwald

"Jüdin"

Häftl.-Nr.: 51246 U

Häftlings-Personal-Karte

Fam.-Name: Königsberg

Vorname:

Geb. am: in: Ungvar

Stand: Kinder:

Wohnort: Ungvar

Strasse:

Religion: Staatsang.: Ungarn

Wohnort d. Angehörigen: Vater: Ferdinand K.,

Eingewiesen am:

durch:

in KL.: Auschwitz

Grund: Polit. Ung. Jüdin

Vorstrafen: Keine

Überstellt

am: 4.10.44 an KL. Buchenwald

am: an KL.

am: an KL.

am: an KL.

am: an KL.

am: an KL.

Entlassung:

am: durch KL.:

mit Verfügung v.:

Personen-Beschreibung:

Grösse: cm

Gestalt:

Gesicht:

Augen:

Nase:

Mund:

Ohren:

Zähne:

Haare:

Sprache:

Bes. Kennzeichen:

Charakt.-Eigenschaften:

Sicherheit b. Einsatz:

Körperliche Verfassung:

Strafen im Lager:

Grund:	Art:	Bemerkung:
Vater:	Mutter:	
Ferdinand K.,	Theodora K., geb.	
	Weinberger	

This is the registration form that was filed out when Rene Konigsberg was sent from Auschwitz Concentration Camp to Essen, Germany, as a slave laborer. (Courtesy of Rene Hammond.)

A German man who worked with them gave one of the women a pair of gloves. "When the SS guard saw it, he grabbed them from the girl, threw it on the fire." Then, he punished her for accepting the gloves.

"This went on all the time. Cruelty was terrible. I remember one SS man used to sit and tell us, 'It doesn't matter who wins the war, we will always have enough time to kill you.'"

They received one meal a day when they returned to the barracks from work—a bowl of soup made from cabbage and potato peelings, and a piece of bread that "looked like a piece of brick." But after a while, even that hard bread began to taste good.

Rene's time in Essen—and her life—was nearly cut short by disease. Soon after arriving, she contracted scarlet fever. Confined to a tent, she lay on straw strewn on the ground with other sick women and women who were pregnant. They were not given any medical care while waiting to be sent back to Auschwitz.

Then one day, her sister, Agnes, came into the tent. "She has that big smile on her face. . . . I said, 'What are you so happy about?' She says, 'We'll be together again.'"

Agnes had gotten sick, too.

But before the Auschwitz transport left, the sisters recovered and were returned to the barracks and to work. It was that love between sisters that Rene believes was at least partially the reason she survived—that and the will to live.

"It was a hard life, but we survived. It's amazing what you can get over, what your body can take."

Because Essen was major industrial area, it was a prime target for British and American bombers. From 1939 to 1945, the city was bombed 272 times, destroying 90 percent of the city center and 60 percent of the rest of the city.[9]

During the bombings, the SS guards took refuge in bomb shelters, while their slave laborers were left exposed to the attack. "We used to stand outside and watch the bombs falling. It was like the Fourth of July, except it was more dangerous."

It was during those raids that the women realized that they could just walk away because nobody was watching them.

But where would they go?

"There were seven German people that worked in the factory and one of them told one of the girls that the war was coming to an end." Gerhard Marquart offered to help them if they could escape.

After the women reached Essen in the late summer of 1944, Marquart had befriended one of the prisoners, Rosa Katz.[10] He smuggled her out of the factory several times so that she could pray at a ruined Jewish cemetery nearby.

Originally, the escape plot involved five prisoners, but a sixth was added because she worked in the kitchen and could provide some food.

The women wanted to escape because "the word was out that they will be taking us back to Auschwitz before the war was finished. And that's one thing that we knew we didn't want."

Their escape was helped by the fact that they had received clothing taken from other Jews. "All we had to do was to take off the yellow star."

"One night [during a bombing raid in February 1945], we said, 'Well, it's tonight or never.'"

Rene and Agnes Konigsberg, sisters Elisabeth and Erna Roth, Rosa Katz, and Gisella Israel set off in search of the cemetery. German civilians they met on the street would ask them if the bombing raid was over because the women were walking away from the bomb shelters. "They thought we were Germans."

When they reached the cemetery, they found the house on the property was in ruins but its cellar was still habitable. And it held cots they could use.

"After our little bit of food that we took with us, we ran out of it, and we said we had to contact the man who said he would help us."

Katz thought she knew where he lived, so one night she and another of the escapees went to find him.

"He was like shocked; he never thought we would actually do it . . . But he kept his word."

Marquart, who lived near the cemetery, "used to bring us boiled potatoes and water every night. He only missed once."

But, a few days after taking refuge in the cellar, a German guard who was watching Russian prisoners of war had discovered the women while he was looking for some missing POWs.

When he asked who they were, "our German was pretty good and so we gave him a story that we were bombed out of our homes and our parents were looking for an apartment."

When Marquart found out, he told the women they had to move because the guard might come back or send others back for them. Initially, they went to Marquart's house, but "it was so close to the front that we could hear shooting."

They were also in danger of being spotted by nearby neighbors.[11] Besides, Marquart did not have enough food to feed them all.[12]

Marquart told them he would find people to help them. And the women remembered another Krupp worker who had promised to help them.[13]

That German could take one of the women, and the other five were sent to Fritz Niermann.[14] He took in Rene, her sister, and the two Roth sisters, while the last escapee found refuge with another German.

Niermann, who ran a wholesale food business, had sent his wife and two daughters to southern Germany to escape the bombing.[15] He and his young housekeeper, Gertrude, took care of the four women. They slept in one of the vacant rooms and Niermann told the women they could wear his daughters' clothing.

"This was the first time we slept in a bed and ate regular food. He had a housekeeper who cooked every day, and he gave us a home, which was also very dangerous [for him]."

As far as their fellow slave laborers at the Krupp factory knew, the six women were dead.

Years after the war, Rene met another Essen survivor in Connecticut who told her about the aftermath of their escape.

Since the prisoners were counted every morning, their absence was discovered the next day. The prisoners were threatened to make them reveal where the escapees had gone. "They didn't know because we didn't tell anybody."

When searchers failed to find them, the guards told the prisoners the six had been caught and shot.

Soon after that, the Jews at the Krupp plant were forced to walk back toward Auschwitz. As Germany collapsed from both west and east, Nazi guards forced concentration camp inmates, Jewish slave laborers, and POWs onto marches to keep them away from advancing Allied and Soviet troops. Many died or were murdered on what became known as Death Marches.

Rene was told the slave laborers from Essen only got as far as Bergen-Belsen Concentration Camp, about 185 miles to the northeast, where typhus was so bad the SS guards refused to go in.

"They just told the girls to go in."

About half of the 500 women survived their ordeal, Rene was told. The camp complex was liberated by British troops on April 15, 1945.[16] Between May 1944 and liberation as many as 37,600 prisoners, including Anne and Margot Frank, died in the camp, while approximately 13,000 more died after liberation because they were too ill to recover. The British burned the camp down to prevent the spread of typhus.

In Essen, Rene and the other escapees stayed hidden for a few weeks. Then, "we noticed that the soldiers on the street didn't wear the same uniform."

American soldiers of the 507th Parachute Infantry Regiment of the U.S. Ninth Army captured Essen on April 11, 1945[17]—bringing Rene and the other women out into the streets to welcome their liberators.

"The Germans looked at us like we were traitors welcoming the enemy, but we were yelling . . . we were liberated."

On March 19, 1985, Gerhard Marquart and Fritz Niermann were recognized by Yad Vashem in Jerusalem as Righteous Among the Nations.[18]

After the war in Europe ended on May 7, 1945, Essen became part of the British zone of occupation. The other zones were occupied by the Americans, French, and Soviets.

"With the three years of English . . . we went to the British military government and we got jobs as interpreters and translators."

It was about this time they had a chance to return home. A Czech officer was putting together a group to return to Czechoslovakia. Rene and Agnes jumped at the chance to go home. But after they signed up to go and left their jobs, came the warning.

"He said, 'Now I have to tell you one thing: No problem going back, but there's no guarantee you can get out again because your home is under the Russian occupation.'"

The sisters had no desire to live under Soviet rule, so they to stayed in Germany.

They went back to work for the British, this time as hostesses in an army officers' club in early 1946.

"It was like being on vacation, really, especially after everything we had been through."

Through their work, they became friendly with some British officers, who offered to help them go to England to work as maids for their families.

"What they were looking for was cheap help. That's the British way. We were not up to that. We had maids in my home, and I didn't want to go and be a maid in somebody else's."

The sisters had not originally wanted to leave Europe, but now they couldn't stay. They started exploring their options since immigration opportunities were opening up for Holocaust survivors. Their choices included such places as the United States, Australia, and New Zealand.

"Definitely, we didn't want to stay in Germany . . . we didn't want to go back to Europe where anti-Semitism was bad."

They thought about going to Chile but relatives there discouraged the sisters, telling them about the anti-Semitism there.

They ruled out going to what was then the British-mandate of Palestine because the British government was trying to keep Jews out, including seizing ships full of Holocaust survivors and interning them in camps on the island of Cyprus.

While they were searching for a place to go to, their brother, Adolf, found them.

After his liberation, Adolf was in one of the many displaced persons camps which had sprung up to care for Holocaust survivors, slave laborers, and others cast adrift at the end of the war.

He had contracted typhus and was not expected to survive. But he did recover and officials wanted to send him to Sweden

This picture of sisters Rene and Agnes Konigsberg, and sisters Elisabeth and Erna Roth was taken in 1946 was of four of the five teenagers who walked away from a slave labor group in Essen, Germany, as World War II came to an end. They managed to stay hidden until liberated by American troops. (Courtesy of Rene Hammond.)

to finish his recuperation, which, Rene said, was common at the time.

He refused. "He said, 'I can't go . . . I promised my father that I'd look after my sisters.'"

So as soon as he felt strong enough, he set off on his quest to find his sisters, visiting DP camps. In one camp, he found survivors of the Essen group. He was told that his sisters had been shot after they were re-captured following their escape.

But no one had seen them shot or had seen their bodies, so Adolf kept searching.

In another DP camp, he met an American official with the United Nations Relief and Rehabilitation Administration, who told him Agnes was working there. That brought the three siblings back together for the first time since the initial selection at Auschwitz, more than a year before.

For Rene, "that was a real miracle that we found each other."

The three siblings decided to try to immigrate to the United States, where immigration for Jews was still tightly restricted.

"Everyone I used to meet in Europe, they said, 'Oh, I have an uncle in New York and he's a millionaire.'"

While her sister stayed in the British zone, Rene and her brother went to Frankfurt, which was in the American occupation zone, to find a way to the United States.

Rene, her sister, and the Rosen sisters needed work. Her brother was supporting himself by buying and selling whatever he could.

Rene went to the offices of the American Jewish Joint Distribution Committee to find a job because none of them wanted to go back to a DP camp. She told the receptionist in the entry hall that they wanted to move to America but first they needed jobs.

"We're not hiring," was the reply.

Rene couldn't accept that, but wasn't sure what to do. Then, she saw the door to the director's office open and somebody came out.

"I ran into him and I told him my story and he says, 'All right, you have that job.'"

"I said, 'Well it is also my sister, and it is also these two other girls.'"

All four landed jobs, moved to the American zone, and registered to come to the United States.

The two sets of sisters shared an apartment, working and waiting for permission to immigrate. Elisabeth and Erna Roth had relatives in the United States who arranged for them to come over. That left Rene and Agnes alone in the Frankfurt apartment, waiting.

In 1947, Rene was invited to a wedding in Heidelberg, about fifty-five miles south of Frankfurt, as a guest of the bride. There she met Ralph Hammond, an American Army soldier from Pennsylvania, who had been invited to the same wedding as a guest of the groom.

After a year of dating, Rene and Ralph married. Ralph wanted to get married in Europe, but Rene wanted to go to America on her own. "I'll see you in the United States," she told him.

But Ralph insisted, so she finally agreed. Later, the couple brought Agnes and Adolf to America, where he spent a career working for Giant supermarkets as a deli manager.

After Ralph was discharged, he went to work driving a bus in Washington, D.C. The couple then moved to Long Island outside of New York City, where he eventually became a plant manager for a garment business.

"He didn't like the cold weather up there," so the couple moved to St. Petersburg, Florida, in 1978, where they opened a gift shop selling jewelry and other items.

Rosa Katz, one of the five girls who walked away from a slave labor camp in Essen, Germany, during a bombing raid. (Courtesy of Rene Hammond.)

Along the way, they raised five children. "And now I have twelve grandchildren and six great-grandchildren."

Of Rene's relatives—aunts, uncles, and cousins—some survived. Some went to the United States and Australia. Some to Israel. One died in the Israeli War of Independence in 1948.

Ralph died in 2003 and Rene moved to a smaller house in 2004 where she now lives. "I didn't want to stay in the house," she said, adding that it had a swimming pool she could not take care of.

Dealing with what happened to her during the war "was difficult at times . . . but the fact that I did have a family helped. But . . . on holidays and remembering what it was like at home . . . your life completely changes. It's nothing like what it was."

Rene has suffered from nightmares as she relived her slice of the Holocaust in her sleep. She would dream her mother survived. "I always hoped that maybe, maybe my mother survived."

Eventually, the dreams faded. "You can't live in the past."

It took time before she could talk to her husband about her experiences. And she didn't tell her children when they were young. "Why burden them with anything like that . . . when they got to be teenagers, they knew about it."

All in all, Rene had what she describes as a normal life after coming to America.

Not every survivor was so lucky.

She has a friend who has had "an unhappy life;" she never managed to "live a normal life."

"She went to Argentina and then the United States." As she was getting older, she feared that she would never have children. "So she married a man who she really didn't love. The marriage was not good."

Her friend has a son and daughter. Her son is a doctor and lawyer, "but not very understanding of what she went through."

Her daughter works to help other people, but Rene's friend feels neglected by her.

"They had a big celebration for [the daughter]. Her mother went. After it was over, she said [to her daughter] she wished 'you would give me half of the attention that you give other people.' So the daughter got mad at that."

Now in the winter of her life, Rene Hammond reflects on her history and experiences.

"I'll tell you, one time somebody interviewed me and he said, 'Do you think that God helped you with your survival?'

"And I thought for a minute, and I said, 'No.' As I said no, he was shocked. And he said, 'Why?'

"I said because why would God help me and not help six million people, little children? My father was a wonderful man; my mother was a wonderful woman. Religious, doing everything that they were supposed to do. And they died. So why would God save me? I couldn't believe it. I don't think God tells you what to do. You're here and you have free will. God did not tell Hitler to kill the people. Hitler was a very nasty man and it wasn't directed by God. At the same time, God does not save you and have you killed.

"I haven't figured it all out . . . but that's one thing that I just couldn't accept."

NOTES

1. JewishGen KehilaLinks, https://kehilalinks.jewishgen.org.
2. JewishGen KehilaLinks.
3. JewishGen KehilaLinks.
4. JewishGen KehilaLinks.
5. JewishGen KehilaLinks.
6. Jewish Virtual Library.
7. JewishGen KehilaLinks.
8. JewishGen KehilaLinks.
9. https://www.essen.de (The city of Essen's website).
10. Yad Vashem.
11. Yad Vashem.
12. Yad Vashem.
13. Yad Vashem.
14. Yad Vashem.
15. Yad Vashem.
16. U.S. Holocaust Memorial Museum, www.ushmm.org.
17. 507th Parachute Infantry Regiment Unit History. https://warfarehistorynetwork.com/daily/wwii/the-507th-parachute-infantry-regiment-in-operation-varsity/.
18. Yad Vashem.

If there really is a God, would he let his people get killed like this? . . . I still don't trust God. I'm still a Jew."

—Gerald Beigel

CHAPTER 4

A BERLINER'S STORY

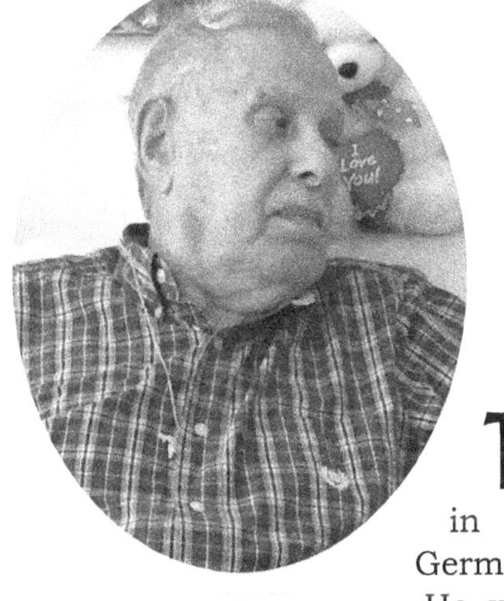

Gerald Beigel

The Jew Gerald Beigel was born February 18, 1928. He grew up in Berlin, the nerve center of Nazi Germany.

He was the second of three children born to Leo and Harte Beigel. Leo was born in 1901 in Posen in what was then eastern Germany, while Harte was born in 1904 in Boyton, Germany, which was on the Polish border at the time.

The couple moved to Berlin where his father worked as a salesman. Their first child, Haust, was born June 1, 1926, followed by Gerald two years later, and finally their daughter, Edit, who was born July 3, 1933.

Gerald and his family had "a lot of non-Jewish friends. They were no different in the beginning."

Those friends proved vital to their survival after Adolf Hitler and his Nazis came to power—and the Beigels and other German Jews had to contend with the growing deadly anti-Semitism Nazis' brought with them.

About 525,000 Jews lived in Germany, which had a total population of 67 million. While Jews made up about .75 of one percent of the population, the Nazis and other anti-Semitic groups blamed them for the nation's ills.

Gerald was born into a nation which had lost the War to End All Wars, a defeat many, if not most, of Germany's citizens were loath to admit was the fault of their army. The loss of World War I was blamed on the "stab in the back"—the myth that the German army was not defeated on the battlefield, but lost the war at home, because of the Jews and others.

The period right after the war was hard on Germans. The Kaiser was gone. A republic, hated by the right and industrialists, had come to power. Communists and Socialists were battling the conservatives and militarists in the streets for power.

By the time Gerald was born, the country was prospering again.

German prosperity, however, was based on heavy borrowing, much of it from American investors, who were being repaid by the British and French for loans made during World War I.

The Germans owed $33 billion to their European foes. That is the equivalent of more than $430 billion today. To pay its reparations and to expand social services, the German Weimar Republic borrowed $7 billion a year from 1924 to 1930. Unemployment was down. Retail sales and industrial output were up.[1]

That didn't help Hitler and his National Socialist Party; there were 108,000 members in 1924 who were the target of jokes when they were mentioned at all. In the 1928 elections, the Nazis got 810,000 votes out of the approximately 31 million cast. They held twelve of the 491 seats in the Reichstag, the German parliament.[2]

Then came October 24, 1929. The American stock market crashed on Wall Street on that Black Tuesday, bringing the Depression, which spread around the world. In Germany, prosperity had been built on foreign loans, most of which came from the United States, and from trade. When those two economic props disappeared, Germany was plunged into economic catastrophe.[3]

The Depression gave Hitler and his Nazis their opening. They gained power by playing on the desperation of the German people. Hitler convinced working people, industrialists, and those in power in the government that only he could rescue them from the unemployment, hunger, and destruction of the economy.[4]

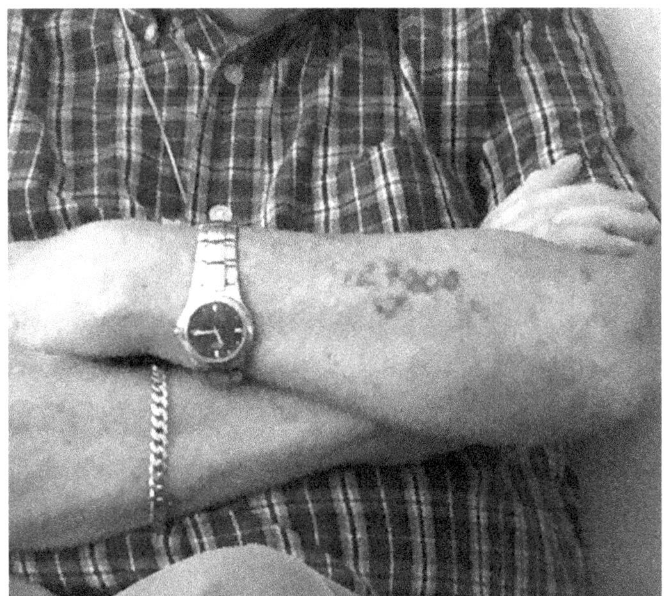

This is the number, 127000, that was tattooed on Gerald's left arm when he became a prisoner in Auschwitz.

In the Reichstag elections of July 31, 1932, the Nazis won 13.7 million votes—more than double their total from two years before, and took 230 seats in the 608-member legislature. Although not a majority, the Nazis were now the largest party and had the support of German's upper and middle classes.[5]

On January 30, 1933, Hitler was appointed chancellor, the leader of the German government, by President Paul von Hindenburg, the revered World War I field marshal.[6]

Any restraint on Hitler's power ended on August 2, 1934, when Hindenburg died at the age of 87. Three hours after the president died, Hitler became head of state and commander-in-chief of the armed forces, under a law the cabinet had enacted on August 1. The office of president was abolished, and Hitler became *Fuhrer*, or Leader, and Reich Chancellor.[7]

Anti-Jewish measures had not waited for Hitler to become all powerful. The Foreign Ministry had been defending German anti-Semitism, and stepped up efforts after January 1933, while later that spring, the Department of Germany was created with the specific assignment to push anti-Semitic propaganda. In March of that year, the city of Cologne barred Jews from using municipal sports facilities. The German Boxing Association kicked out all Jewish boxers on April 4, and on April 8, the universities in the state of Baden fired all Jewish teaching assistants.

—

In 1933, Jews could no longer hold public office or serve in the civil services; they could not be in journalism, radio, farming, teaching, or the performing arts.[8]

—

In 1934, Jews were banned from working in stock exchanges.[9]

The most infamous anti-Semitic legislation was the Nuremberg Laws of September 15, 1935. Jews were stripped of their German citizenship; marriage between Jews and "Aryans" was forbidden, as were sexual relations; and Jews could not employ "Aryan" female servants younger than thirty-five years old. Over the next few years, a series of thirteen decrees so restricted Jewish life that by 1936 most had no way of making a living. Then, in 1938, a decree which had been announced in 1934, took effect which prevented Jews from practicing medicine or the law or being in business.[10]

—

During the 1930s, Jewish businesses were boycotted before they were banned, and violence against Jews flared repeatedly around the country.

That violence reached a crescendo on the night of November 9 to 10, 1938, during the Kristallnacht pogrom, so called because of the broken glass from windows in homes, businesses, and synagogues which littered the streets. The excuse was the November 7 fatal shooting of Ernst vom Rath, the third secretary of the German Embassy in Paris. The attacker was Herschel Grynszpan, a seventeen-year-old German Jewish refugee, upset that his father had been deported to Poland along with 10,000 other Jews. At the time of his death, the Gestapo was investigating Vom Rath for his anti-Nazi views: He did not share their anti-Semitic beliefs.[11]

In the well-organized, "spontaneous" pogrom, more than 100 Jewish men, women, and children were killed, and at least that many more were injured, according to the Nazis' own figures. Hundreds of businesses and homes were set on fire or destroyed, 119 synagogues were set on fire and 76 were destroyed, and 20,000 Jews were arrested. A number of rapes were reported and 7,500 Jewish shops were looted. Those who committed rape were expelled from the Nazi party and turned over to the courts for violating the law banning sexual relations with Jews. Nothing happened to those who murdered Jews.[12]

Kristallnacht, as it turned out, was only the beginning.

For Gerald and his family, life had become precarious and limited.

"We were not allowed to go to the movies. Some of my friends took me." That had a certain amount of risk. "When somebody said there's a Jew in the movie, they beat them up."

Gerald started school in 1932. The Jewish schools were all full, so his mother enrolled him in the local neighborhood school. He was the only Jew in his class, possibly the only Jew in the school.

The teacher put the six-year-old in a corner of the room. He received special treatment: Whenever he didn't know the answer to a question, he was beaten.

He only stayed in that school for one semester. "My mother asked me how was the school, [then] put me in another school. But it was the same thing."

The next year, seven-year-old Gerald went to second grade in an orphanage which had been converted to a Jewish school. "I was there maybe three years, and then [the government] needed the land and they sent me to another school. It was closer [to home], at least."

The last couple of years he was in that school, he was able to ride his bicycle to class.

The next Jewish school he attended had to close after he was there for two years when the government took the building to be used as a warehouse. The next school, which he attended for half a year, also closed when the government took the property.

At this point, Gerald and his siblings could not attend public schools—on November 15, 1938, all Jews were ordered expelled from German schools.[13]

In 1941, when he turned thirteen, Gerald was ordered to go to work. "My parents told me not to work like in shoveling snow and working in a factory. . . . They got me a job." That job had him working in a Jewish cemetery cutting up metal railings for the army.

His father, who was no longer allowed to work in business, was forced by the Nazis to build railroads at night.

—

In early 1941, Berlin was home to about 74,500 Jews. By October 1, 350 had left; then on October 18, the Nazis banned further Jewish emigration. In September 1941, Germany's Jews were ordered to wear a yellow Star of David with the word "Jude" on it. They now were easy targets for abuse or deportation to the east, which, for most of them, was a death sentence.[14] The stars cost ten pfennig, or about one dollar, each.

On October 1, 1941, Yom Kippur—the holiest day of the Jewish year—the Gestapo in Berlin pulled the community's three top officials—President Moritz Henschel, his deputy, Philip Kotzover, and the director of the housing office, Martha Mosse—out of services to tell them many of the Jews who were still in Berlin were to be deported. They were ordered to immediately submit up-to-date lists of the city's Jews with their addresses. They were also ordered to turn the Levetzow Street synagogue into a transit camp for 1,000 deportees. Later, other deportation sites were set up in a Jewish home for the aged, the community office building, and the Jewish hospital.[15]

The Nazis deported the Jews in stages. The now fourteen-year-old Gerald and his family had their turn in the spring of 1942.

"One day I came home from work," and standing on the corner was one of his neighbors, who warned him, "'Don't go home. The Gestapo is waiting for you.'"

No one in the family was home when the Gestapo arrived to pick them up. Their Christian neighbors staked out the four corners of the block around the house to warn each one as they came home.

Gerald was told to go to an apartment that was not too far away to meet the rest of his family.

"We stayed there a couple of days, and then we couldn't stay there too long because if you stayed too long they know that's not somebody's home. In Berlin, in Germany, if you moved from one apartment to next door, you have to go to the police station and sign in."

Because of the danger to themselves and the non-Jews who were hiding them, the family split up. Gerald's parents and sister stayed together, but he and his brother hid in different places, moving constantly.

"I lived with all kinds of different people." When he wasn't sleeping in someone's apartment, he was walking the streets of

Berlin. Since he wasn't wearing a yellow star, he was able to blend in. To get indoors, he sometimes went to the movies.

Despite the constant moving, the family members were able to stay in touch. "I went to find my parents to get food."

That quest for food got Gerald caught—not as a Jew, but as a person dealing in the black market.

In February 1943—the family had been hiding for nearly a year—Gerald met his mother and sister at a butcher's shop, a place the family members had often gone. "I meet my mother, they give me food to take home to where I live." The police arrived before they could disperse, ready to arrest everyone. "My sister said she has to go to the bathroom. My mother took her and they disappeared" by climbing out the bathroom window.

Harte Beigel and her daughter, Edit, remained free for more than two years more before they were caught, and sent to Auschwitz, where they were gassed as soon as they arrived. Harte was forty-one. Edit was thirteen. His father, who was caught at the same time, survived.

While Gerald and his family had many non-Jewish friends who hid them, it was "Jews [who] killed them. Some of the Jews point out the Jews" in deals with the Nazis in an attempt to save their own lives and those of their families.

Gerald believes his parents and sister were denounced by one of those Jews. Stella Goldschlag, a Berlin Jew, had been in hiding with her parents using false papers. When they were caught, she struck a deal with the Germans—she would help them find other hidden Jews if they would not transport her or her parents. The Germans agreed, but in February 1944, her parents were sent to Theresienstadt Concentration Camp and then to Auschwitz, where they were killed.

As for Stella Goldschlag, she is blamed for getting hundreds of Jews caught by the Nazis. After the war, she was taken into custody by the Soviets, identified as a Nazi collaborator by other Jews, and sentenced to ten years in prison. She was released in 1956. She committed suicide in 1994.[16]

Because Gerald was arrested for black-market activities and not as a Jew, the teenager was taken to a civilian jail, where he was locked up in a room with 400 other prisoners. "All of them slept on top of each other. All of them facing criminal charges." Polish soldiers also were being held in the jail.

This photograph of Gerald Beigel, left, his father, Leo, and brother, Haust, was taken after the war. (Courtesy of Gerald Beigel.)

As a matter of routine, police had taken Gerald's fingerprints but it would be four months before he was identified as a Jew.

At first, he went on work details like everyone else in the jail. "Then I talked to the guy in charge. He was a Jewish guy." He had been a colonel in the Belgian army, "but he spoke five languages so [the Germans] kept him in charge" of the jail. "He got me out of there," setting him to work peeling potatoes, some of which supplemented Gerald's jailhouse diet.

Then, he and four other Jews were sent to work in a women's jail which was being built. Their job was to put wires on windows. While the Belgian colonel knew they were all Jews, the Germans didn't.

Every morning, the five Jews were picked up at the jail by a special bus and taken to the work site. The route took them by where his parents were in hiding, "every morning, every night." For the month that they were on that detail, their living conditions improved, with the five of them sharing one room, instead of being with 400 others.

In May 1943, Gerald's fingerprints came back—and he was identified as a Jew. "They sent me to Gestapo headquarters. They knew my parents were still out there someplace so they wanted to know where they are. I said, 'I had no idea. I never lived with them for a long time.' So they beat me up."

After the Gestapo agents gave up questioning him, Gerald was put with other Jews waiting to be sent to Auschwitz. All the while, Gerald was waiting for an opportunity to escape. "I had a good chance to run away." Then, the Germans asked him his name and immediately put him in handcuffs. It turned out that his brother, Haust, had been captured earlier and had escaped.

Eventually, Haust was caught a second time, and this time the Nazis held on to him. The brothers were reunited at the Berlin collection center where Jews who had been captured were awaiting transport to Auschwitz. They were there a few days before being loaded onto a truck and taken to the train station, where they were put in boxcars headed to the concentration camp.

"One of the guys had a saw, a little saw." They started trying to cut a way out but were caught by an SS guard.

When they reached Auschwitz in April 1943, "the guy with the saw was sent to the gas. They didn't want to kill all of us . . . there were eighteen-year-old boys, nineteen-year-old guys." But Gerald "was small for my age and I was fifteen years old."

During the initial selection in the detraining area, "with a finger they put my brother to the right and me to the left. And I automatically went to my brother's side or I would have been gassed."

Instead, Gerald became prisoner number 127000—a number he still carries tattooed on his left forearm today.

When they were processed in, "the only thing we could keep were the shoes when we changed clothes," putting on the striped jail uniform. "I had a good pair of shoes," which he was told to put on the floor next to the bunks where they slept. In the morning, all the shoes were gone.

"I complained, four of us complained, 'What happened to our shoes?'" The result was they were forced to do pushups. "I never got my shoes back. Instead . . . we got wooden shoes. You couldn't even walk a block; you got stuck in the mud with the shoes. Anyway, after a couple of days . . . I saw a few dead people. I took the shoes from the dead people . . . So I had shoes at least. . . . That's how you live there."

"All we had for breakfast . . . [was] some water that they called tea with some leaves in there . . . for lunch, we had some watery soup, what they called soup—just water with some green stuff in there. At night, we had a slice of bread and sometimes you have small piece of cheese. That was our food."

Shortly after arriving, "we had another selection . . . it was a small group of German Jews" who were to be trained as bricklayers. "They put us in one block . . . we live in this building. On top of this building, on the top floor, they showed us how to lay bricks. After a few months . . . they sent us out to build. But instead of building, all we did was mix cement, carry bricks up the ladder [to where others were laying bricks], carry cement up the ladder, and that's all we did."

At the end of the workday, the prisoners were marched back to their barracks where they were counted.

In the concentration camp, "I met a lot of my friends I went to school with, even teachers . . . None of them made it." They had all been caught in 1942, while Gerald and his family were still being sought by the Gestapo. "That one year in underground saved my life, saved my brother's life."

But a urinary tract infection nearly proved fatal for Gerald. "I couldn't pee for a while, so I went to . . . what we called a hospital."

His medical problem drew the attention of Dr. Josef Mengele, a member of the SS who became infamous for performing deadly experiments on inmates. The doctor ran a tube through his stomach to study Gerald's condition.

A Czechoslovakian doctor saved Gerald. "Every time Mengele came to the hospital, he was hiding me under the bed and I made it." The doctor couldn't save all the patients, so he picked ones for whom there was hope. "I was a young kid and all the others were over fifty and were already half dead. I was only a quarter dead."

As the Red Army drove west, entering Budapest in Hungary and taking Warsaw in Poland on January 17, 1945, Auschwitz and other concentration camps became vulnerable to capture by the Soviets.

All through the crumbling Nazi empire, concentration camp inmates, prisoners of war, and other victims of the Germans were being driven west to keep them from being liberated by the Red Army. At this point, the Soviets had driven Germany's Romanian, Bulgarian, and Hungarian allies from the war. In the west, the Anglo-American armies had broken the back of the Wehrmacht, the German army, following the Battle of the Bulge which began in December 1944. It was the last major offensive the Germans would launch. But the Allies did not cross the Rhine River, the last major natural obstacle into Germany, until March 1945. The

German army still had some fight left, but it had become clear to all except the most fanatical Nazis that the end was near.

The evacuation of the Auschwitz-Birkenau complex had started as much as four months earlier, with prisoners taken west in the fall of 1944. But approximately 64,000 prisoners were still in Auschwitz on January 18, 1945—within earshot of Russian artillery—when the final evacuation order was issued.[17]

The inmates, starving and poorly clothed, many of whom were sick, were marched out on foot. Some were loaded onto rail cars headed to western Germany and away from liberation. Others were forced to march hundreds of miles to the west, on deadly journeys often taking a month.[18]

Gerald and his brother were among the inmates driven out of Auschwitz, while his father came out of nearby Birkenau.

Thousands died on the journey, from exposure, from exhaustion, and, if they couldn't keep up, from being shot by their guards. Those who tried to escape were shot. They received little food or water as they walked along in their prison pajamas in the January cold.

Gerald, who had lost touch with his brother, was among tens of thousands of prisoners who were marched out in January 1945. His group headed northwest: Destination, Gross-Rosen Concentration Camp, near Breslau. He and his father found each other among the thousands of Jews, Russians, and Poles, as well as other nationalities, who were being stuffed into the camp from other places.

It was a dangerous place. "When we went to get soup, we had to pass by not far from the wires."

Other prisoners would push "you into the wires and take the food. People were fighting for survival and they don't mind killing other people to get it."

After two or three nights in the camp, "they line us up. All my friends were lining up and I found my father, he was next to me. And I never saw [again] any of my friends who were in front of me."

About an hour after they were lined up, they were loaded onto open train cars to move to western Germany. "This was winter time. Snow." During the trip to Buchenwald, which is near Weimar, Germany, some of the prisoners froze to death. Gerald and his father "were lucky."

As the train stopped, the prisoners found themselves in the middle of an air raid. "The plane came. The American plane. And they threw down bombs like anything. They didn't know who was there. It was a big railway station. They didn't see from upstairs who was there. They just bombed it. A lot of Germans got killed there, too; a lot of Jews got killed there."

In the camp itself, "we were lying there . . . for five days before we got something to eat. Too many people came there."

A week had gone by when "they told us: Anybody wants more soup? . . . I went. My father stayed." Gerald and other inmates were put on a train headed for southern Germany "to make a hole in the mountain, I think for the atomic bomb." The Germans, as well as the Americans and British, had been working on developing atomic weapons. While the German effort had failed, the Americans were close to perfecting the new weapon, although the first test was not conducted until July 16, 1945, after Germany surrendered in May.

Two shifts were digging what may have been a bomb shelter for the Nazis, but more probably was for an underground munitions factory or some other such facility. One shift was comprised of Jewish concentration camp inmates, and other "undesirables;" the other, Jewish-American POWs.

Gerald was spared from the digging. When he got there, he met a cousin, Udel Schwartz, who had been in Birkenau and was now one of the prisoners responsible for food distribution.

Gerald went to work in the kitchen. He was told by his cousin and others that his brother had been shot and killed while trying to escape during a Death March that had left Auschwitz in September 1944.

After a couple of months, Gerald and his fellow prisoners were put on another Death March. This time to Mauthausen Concentration Camp, in southwest Germany. Again, he knew someone who was in charge of food distribution, "so I had no problem getting food there. But I never went to work. I had a hiding place in the barracks." That could be dangerous because SS guards would periodically search for inmates who were hiding.

Then one day, "the SS came around and I heard somebody say . . . this SS needed some people for the civil kitchen." They were speaking in German. "I understood; I volunteered."

The SS troops took Gerald and another prisoner to the civilian kitchen "where we were cleaning pots and had plenty of food."

"But I got hurt there." A large, hot pot fell on his leg. The injury soon became infected. "They put me in sick bay," which had a grass floor. He was among six or seven other people there. "There was no care, no nothing. There were no doctors." His medical care consisted of him tearing a piccc of his shirt to drain the pus from his infected leg.

As he was lying there, the Germans decided to move their prisoners further west to the Dachau Concentration Camp.

"My cousin . . . came and said, 'You cannot stay here . . . they will shoot you.' I said I couldn't even stand up. 'No problem, we'll stand you up,' [he said]."

But Gerald was too weak to stand, so he was left lying on the ground when they marched out. What saved him was that the Nazis "did not want to leave dead people behind." So he and the others were carried out and put on the train.

"We came to Dachau and they put me in a cabin and I was lying with two dead people. So after a couple of days, they picked us up and put us on a pushcart to be burned. . . . Somebody outside said, 'There's somebody moving,' so they took me off the truck."

His fellow inmates gave him some water. He was running a high temperature as his weakened body fought the infection in his leg. "Then they get me something to eat. They got some food once a day so they give me some, and I feel better."

It was in April 1945, shortly before Adolf Hitler died on April 30. The SS decided to move their prisoners again. This time the destination was further south, to Innsbruck, Austria.

About 1,000 inmates, guarded by mostly Ukrainian and some Polish members of the SS, reached the border only to be surrounded by Austrian border police. They were told "we can't go to Austria; we have to go back to Germany."

So they started walking back into Germany, with Gerald being helped by a couple of the others. They had gone about a mile or a bit more, and as it was getting dark, "a troop of SS came, with cars, with trucks, with everything."

They were on the highway running through a valley. Next to the road were railroad tracks and on the other side of those was a mountain. On the other side of the highway was a stream, then a grassy area with some stones, next a small river, and finally the mountains.

The SS troops pushed the Jews to the side of the road. "They started to shoot, but they didn't shoot so good."

Gerald and some others were able to escape. "A couple of my friends from Auschwitz, they took me up the mountains." There

Gerald Beigel and his wife, Ellen. (Courtesy of Gerald Beigel.)

they found a ski cabin, full of German soldiers hiding from the SS, who would have shot them as deserters. "They gave us something to eat," and uniforms to replace their prison pajamas.

The trio stayed there for a day, and then ventured back to the scene of the shooting. The SS had left. Hundreds of dead Jews were lying there. "They made it the whole time in the camps, and they come to the end of the camps, and they get killed by some stupid SS. Hitler was dead already."

The trio started walking, with Gerald being helped by his two companions. They walked north, finding no food along the way. "You eat nothing for a week. That means nothing. Then you eat grass."

As they were headed for an American refugee collection center, they heard shooting and went to investigate. A woman, who was living on the first floor, said a German officer in charge of a labor camp and his family were living upstairs. When they went upstairs, they found the officer had shot and killed his wife and baby, and then committed suicide.

"My two friends threw [the bodies] out of the window."

They stayed there a few days. Every morning the woman downstairs cooked hot cereal for him.

"I was 83 or 80 pounds because I didn't eat nothing for a while. . . . She cooked very good and I gained weight very fast."

Along the way to the American center, the trio got rid of the uniforms they had been given by the German soldiers, putting on civilian clothes.

When they reached the American camp, Gerald was put in a mobile aid station for treatment.

"The doctor said they cannot save the leg. They had to cut the leg. I said . . . after all I've been through, I don't want to live without the leg . . . they clean it out and fixed it the best they could . . . then they told me they can do nothing but they give me an injection."

The treatment worked. After about two weeks, his leg was healed enough for him to go to a Displaced Persons Camp near Garmisch, in Bavaria.

The European war, by this time, was over.

Gerald was seventeen years old and alone. He didn't know if his father had survived. He had been told his brother was dead, as were his mother and sister.

In the DP camp, he was approached by a recruiter for the *Haganah*—"The Defense" in English—a Jewish paramilitary force that had been formed in the wake of Arab riots and violence targeting Jews in Palestine which the British, who ruled the area, were doing little to prevent. As Jews sought to establish their own state in Palestine, the Haganah became vital for self-defense. The organization became the core of the Israeli Defense Force after Israel was founded in 1948.

This recruiter had been born in Berlin but emigrated to Britain before the war. He had joined the British Army's Jewish Brigade, which was composed mostly of Palestinian Jews.

Gerald signed up to go to Palestine. But there was no way to get there just yet since the British were doing all they could to keep Jews out in their effort to appease Arab public opinion.

The same recruiter went to another American-run DP camp in Landsberg, which also was in Bavaria. Through the recruiter's talking to people there, Leo Beigel found out that at least one of his sons had survived.

Gerald, however, still didn't know about his father. "After a few months in Garmisch, I went to different DP camps to see who survived. As I was walking in [to the Landsberg DP camp], my father was walking out. Small world."

They went back to Garmisch. "I had already lived in a house in a couple of rooms with survivors."

But after several weeks there, Leo wanted to return to Berlin to find out who survived. So his father headed north, while Gerald stayed, saying he would wait for his father to pick him up. "I was seventeen. My father was forty-four." He had made his father promise to come back for him.

Every week for a month, Gerald would wait at the station for the train from Munich for his father to return. Leo never came back.

Instead, his "dead" brother, Haust, got off the train. Haust and their father had found each other in Berlin. His father stayed there, while Haust came back for Gerald.

"He was only one of a couple of people who made it [from the Death March] . . . He made it all the way to Berlin [from Auschwitz], 300 miles. He stole clothes . . . on the way, and changed his striped clothes. He made believe he was hurt in the [German] army. He was a survivor, you know."

The brothers stayed in Garmisch for a time, until Haust suggested they return to Berlin where their father was waiting for them. Although he had signed up to go to Palestine, Gerald wanted to see his father.

By now it was the end of 1946 and going to Berlin was not an easy undertaking. After the German surrender, the country had been divided into four occupation zones: Soviet in the east, British in the northwest, American in the south, and French in the southwest. Moving between the Soviet zone and the others was not a simple matter because the Russians regulated travel. And Berlin was in the Soviet zone.

The brothers and four others hired a man to drive them to Berlin from the American zone. They didn't get far over the border. "We heard shooting, they were shooting over our heads. The Russians came and put us in jail."

In jail, Gerald heard one Soviet officer talking to another in Yiddish. He asked the officer if he was a "yid." When the officer said yes, Gerald told him their story. "He gave us something to eat; the next day, he took us in a car to the station" and got them on a train to Berlin.

"Sometimes you have a miracle."

The boys found their father, and the three of them started life again in Berlin. "My father found a girlfriend . . . she was forty-one years old. A *shiksa* [non-Jewish woman] who was married to [a German] officer who got killed in the war."

While in Berlin, Gerald went to the headquarters for Jewish agencies. "And who's sitting there? One of the Auschwitz *kapos.*" He was one of the main supervisors in that office. [The Germans appointed the Jews to supervise other Jewish prisoners. The SS expected a kapo to be brutal toward other prisoners. If he wasn't, he was returned to normal prisoner status, losing his authority and privileges.]

"I said 'What the heck are you doing here? Your nephew died. He came to you for a little soup. You wouldn't give him a little soup. You could eat how much you wanted. You let him die.'"

The former kapo told Gerald he wouldn't be able to accomplish anything in Berlin.

"I said, 'Oh, yes?' So I made a big issue in the headquarters of the Jewish organization. He went to South Africa."

One thing did change: Gerald's travel plans. "I had signed up for Israel," but his father "made me go to America. He had a brother who was in America."

The day came in 1946 when the three of them were to leave for New York. They were each allowed to take one suitcase and five dollars, the equivalent of $67.73 in 2018. They took a train to a north German port where they were to board their ship the next day. They spent the night in a hostel.

When Gerald and Haust got ready to go the next morning, their father wasn't there. "Me and my brother looked for my father. We find him on the train going back to Berlin. He liked the girlfriend."

The brothers were having none of that. "We caught my father, we took him off, and we took the ship to America."

"He made me go to America . . . I had signed up for Israel."

When they reached New York, the American Jewish Joint Distribution Committee offered to help them. Gerald was seventeen and Haust was nineteen. All three of them were unemployed and had no money.

The Jewish agency "came and said, 'Look, we're going to put you through school . . . your father, we're going to get you an apartment and we're going to get you a job.'

"My father said, 'We don't take welfare.'"

They moved in with Leo's brother, Gerhardt Beigel, who had room in his apartment in the Brooklyn neighborhood of Washington Heights—a fifth-floor walkup. "His daughter had just got married. His son died serving with the U.S. Army in Europe. He wasn't even really a [U.S.] citizen . . . [but he spoke] German."

Gerald's uncle knew the owner of Block Handbags and got the boys jobs cleaning the factory.

His father eventually opened a cleaning store which he later sold and went to work for other companies. He eventually remarried. "He had plenty of money and he lived happy" the rest of his life. Leo Beigel died in 1969.

—

A week after he was in America, Gerald was working as a janitor. "I got paid $25" a week. After taxes, he took home $21. "I paid my uncle $18 [in rent.] . . . My brother paid $18; it was $18 for my father, too."

—

After six months at the factory, the boys had to join the union if they were going to stay. Gerald stayed. Haust didn't.

Instead, Haust and a friend of his went to Florida. The two launched careers as beach boys. The friend's uncle owned a hotel in Miami so he gave them odd jobs. Next, Haust drove cars to New York for people, then sold stoves in the 1950s before making "a couple of million dollars" in commercial real estate. He married and had a family. Haust Beigel died in 2008.

Haust was the first to move out of Gerhardt's apartment when he went to Florida. Then, his father got a girlfriend and moved out.

"I got stuck with my uncle for another couple of months. Then I moved . . . into a rooming house in between Westside Avenue and 97th Street." The rooming house was home to a lot of refugees, including the woman he would marry.

Ellen was born on July 7, 1926, in Germany. "I was a year and a half younger than she was. But I was older. When I was 17 years old, I was like an old man already."

Ellen's parents had gotten her a visa to come to the United States. They had tried to get her to Britain, but that avenue was closed by the war. So were the usual routes over the Atlantic.

When she was 14 years old, she came to the United States by crossing Siberia and going through Korea and China, before sailing to the safety of America. Her parents could not get out and did not survive the war.

Ellen was with a lot of other Jews on the train trip through Siberia. The Russians made them keep the blinds down—they weren't allowed to look out the windows. She was the only child on that train who was able to go to America. The others went to China and other places.

Her first job, at the age of fourteen, was working as a maid in Albany, New York. After she graduated from high school, she went to work in a delicatessen. When she had saved enough money, she moved to New York City, where she knew someone.

The couple married in 1949 and had two children. Ellen died in 2014.

While he was living in the rooming house, Gerald was still working as a janitor of the company that made high-end handbags. But he didn't stay a janitor. "At the end I was the vice president of the company. When I started, it had twelve people working. When I quit, we had 125 people."

He quit because "my boss went and sold the place, and sold it with me. And I walked out. I said that I wasn't for sale." He had some job offers already, so he took a summer vacation before starting a new job, and after working for several more handbag companies, he retired at the age of 59 following a bout of colon cancer.

—

Today, Gerald lives in comfortable retirement in Florida.

His experiences in the Holocaust leave him skeptical about religion. The Holocaust has left its mark on him. While he holds onto his Judaism, he is skeptical about religion, and about God.

"If there really is a God, would he let the people get killed like this? Let's be honest, six million people. Would he let them be killed? Let them be killed in front of everybody in the whole world? I mean, come on. I still don't trust God. I'm still a Jew."

NOTES

1. Shirer, *The Rise and Fall*, 117.
2. Shirer, *The Rise and Fall*, 118.
3. Shirer, *The Rise and Fall*, 135–136.
4. Shirer, *The Rise and Fall*, 135.
5. Shirer, *The Rise and Fall*, 166.
6. Shirer, *The Rise and Fall*, 4.
7. Shirer, *The Rise and Fall*, 226.
8. Shirer, *The Rise and Fall*, 233.
9. Shirer, *The Rise and Fall*, 233.
10. Shirer, *The Rise and Fall*, 233.
11. Shirer, *The Rise and Fall*, 430.
12. Shirer, *The Rise and Fall*, 431.

13. Saul Friedlander, *Nazi Germany and the Jews*, no. 1 (n.p.: HarperCollins Publishers. 1997): 284.

14. David J. Hogan, Editor-in-Chief, *The Holocaust Chronicle* (n.p.: Publications International Ltd): 268.

15. Holocaust Education and Archive Research Team.

16. Shlomit Lasky and Maayan Meyer, https://www.aviva-berlin.de, August 2018.

17. Reitlinger, *The Final Solution: The Attempt*, 457–458.

18. Gilbert, *The Holocaust: A History*, 770.

"How could anyone have feelings about God with what was going on? Where was He when we needed Him?"
—Bonnie Kahane

CHAPTER 5

SOLE SURVIVOR

Bonnie Kahane, formerly Bronia Hoffman

Moshe Hoffman was a commodity broker, buying and selling grain and produce from farmers, in what was then southeastern Poland. Today it is part of Ukraine.

Moshe worked with his father, Yosef Hoffman, and Mendel Frankel, the brother of his wife, Chana.

Moshe, or Morris, was born in 1900. Chana, or Anna, Frankel was three years younger, born in 1903. They lived, worked, and died, in Buczacz, the birthplace of Simon Wiesenthal, who survived the Holocaust to become a world-famous Nazi hunter.

The couple survived World War I when the Austrian-Hungarian Empire joined Germany in defeat. In the aftermath of that war, the Empire was carved up into its component parts, with Poland regaining its independence. But the end of the First World War didn't bring peace to all of eastern Europe. In 1920-21, the Soviet-Polish War was fought. During that struggle, a Ukrainian army occupied Buczacz, murdering and raping Jews.[1]

In the later 1920s and 1930s, life had settled down with the creation of a Jewish bank, as well as Jewish schools. Associations of Jewish merchants and craftsmen were formed in the area which was overwhelmingly Ukrainian.[2] Poles and Jews were distinct minorities.

—

On April 17, 1931, Moshe and Chana Hoffman had a daughter, Bronia, or Bonnie. In 1935, their son, Julius, or Jully, was born.

Because of Moshe's business, at which Chana also worked, the family lived in a house on Pod-Zamek Street, about half a mile outside of Buczacz, home to about 10,000 Jews.[3] They also employed a maid.

For young Bronia, life was good. She played with other children, and eventually started the first grade, an education that would also end there. She got along well with her Ukrainian neighbors.

The family was observant but "we weren't fanatic. . . . My father wore a yarmulke. We kept kosher homes, you know. My grandfather wore a beard. He was reading the Holy Book every Saturday afternoon."

Moshe and Chana Hoffman were able to make a living during the years of turmoil of the worldwide Great Depression and the rise of Nazi Germany to the west of Poland and the Union of Soviet Socialist Republics to the east of the country. As German Fuhrer Adolf Hitler prepared to invade Poland, he needed to keep the Soviet Union out of the fighting. While he eventually planned to invade the USSR, he wasn't ready to do that yet. First, he wanted to deal with Poland, and possibly France and Britain, if they came into the war. On August 23, 1939, Germany and the Soviet Union signed a non-aggression treaty.[4]

Germany provoked World War II with the invasion of Poland on September 1, 1939. A little more than two weeks later, the Soviet Red Army launched its invasion of eastern Poland on September 17.

Twenty days later, it was all over, and Poland ceased to exist as an independent nation. Buczacz was now part of the Soviet Union.[5]

Bronia "didn't feel the difference." But her parents did. "My father was immediately out of business and I only remember my father used to be always in the kitchen," something she had never

Bronia with her mother, Chana Hoffman, in the 1930s. (Courtesy of Bonnie Kahane.)

seen before. He couldn't work; he couldn't safely leave the house. Her mother kept the family going by selling vegetables from their garden and doing other business. Chana spoke Ukrainian and Polish and would dress like a non-Jew when she left the house, giving her relative freedom of movement.

The Soviets abolished all the Jewish organizations, including schools, and all private businesses were nationalized. Thousands of Jews from Nazi-occupied western Poland fled east, many reaching what was then the safety of Buczacz. Then, in June 1940, the Soviets deported hundreds of the city's Jews to the Gulag, the Soviet Union's system of punishment camps where people who were accused of real or imagined political or criminal crimes were forced into slave labor.[6]

At least some of the food Bronia's family relied on came from the two-acre garden her mother took care of. Her parents also began selling what they owned to provide for necessities.

Bronia is not sure how her parents managed under Soviet occupation. "I only knew that come lunchtime, I have food on the table."

The relative safety of Buczacz ended when the German army, the Wehrmacht, launched Operation Barbarossa, the invasion of the Soviet Union, on June 22, 1941. The Red Army immediately drafted some Jews, while other young Jews fled east into the Soviet interior.[7]

"That's when problems started. . . . There were 10,000 Jews in our town and by the time [the Germans] got finished, less than 100 remained."

Even before the Germans occupied Buczacz on July 7, the killing of Jews had begun. Ukrainian nationalists had been attacking Jews, killing a number of them.[8]

Within a week of the German occupation, "they had a rally; in the center of it was a big hill [Fedor Hill], a get-together place, and the Germans gave [the Ukrainians] a pep talk. The Jews didn't go to the rally. [The Germans] just invited . . . the troublemakers." The Ukrainians were told they could take whatever they wanted from Jews.

And that is what happened: Jewish property was looted and some Jews were shot.

"We know it's going to be trouble. My mother closes the [house's] shutters. And somebody knocked on the shutters. It was from an across-the-street neighbor and she opened up. She figured she's going to tell her what's from the rally. The first thing that came out of [the neighbor's] mouth was 'This is what we're going to do to you,'" and she made a cutting motion with her finger across her throat.

"My mother shut the shutter fast. And then, after that, it was downhill fast."

In town, where the synagogue was, Jews were pulled off the street and killed. "They started shooting this one, killing this one, beating up another one. We were still not touched."

Two weeks after the Nazis' arrival, Ukrainian police pulled about forty Jews and non-Jews from the city's prison, and along with two Gestapo officials, took them to the nearby Lezniczowska Forest. The prisoners were ordered to undress; then, they were robbed, abused, and murdered with machine guns and hand grenades.[9]

On August 26, 1941, the Germans ordered Jewish men between the ages of 18 and 50 to register. Those who showed up were taken to a local prison. A number of craftsmen were released. The rest—between 350 and 450—were held overnight. In the morning, they were taken to Fedor Hill and shot by Ukrainian auxiliaries who had been trained by Einsatzgruppen C, one of the German death squads which followed the army with the assignment to kill Jews. The men were buried in pits that had already been dug.[10]

The Germans were targeting "young people, 300 professionals and college-material professionals mostly. . . . What they did is they took and shot them immediately, so there was nobody to lead."

Within a month of the Nazis' arrival, the Hoffman family had to move into town. "My mother found a place . . . and that's where we went. It was one room. . . . They tell you, 'You just take what you could carry.' How much can you carry? We took a sheet, put in stuff, bedding, whatever. That was it."

When the Hoffmans left their home, "people were standing there to take over the place."

The Germans had conscripted Moshe Hoffman's brother for forced labor, putting him in a work camp to build roads. "He was a bookkeeper. . . . They had to chop [rocks] up and put it into roads."

After her uncle was in the camp for a month, a new regulation allowed substitutions. "My father felt bad for him so he went and changed it with him and my uncle came to us. . . . His hands were bleeding."

"We knew there was going to be another action and we had no place to go. So, what happened was my aunt asked what we are going to do. My mother says, 'Nothing. I'm going to stay in the house.' We didn't know . . . how things were going to work out."

Just before the action, Chana Hoffman moved a loose board leading to the attic. "She took the table over and she went up to see. She made like bedding for us and she pushed us up, my brother, myself, and she climbed up. . . . She took up some things for drinking, for eating, and we stayed up there." Their Polish

Bronia and her mother, Chana Hoffman, in the 1930s. (Courtesy of Bonnie Kahane.)

landlady "pulled away the table." Bronia's uncle "went back to my aunt's house."

On October 17, 1942, the Germans launched an action. "We heard shooting . . . we were very quiet, and somebody opened the door and we heard shooting in the house. . . . Then, all of a sudden my mother heard my aunt running in . . . and the Germans were behind her and the police. They shot them by us in the street." The Germans took the bodies away.

"Then the Polish woman came and said everything is over." The three of them got down.

"That was the beginning of it. That was the first shock that we had, and then, of course, my father was not with us."

Her uncle, who had survived the action, did not want to go back to the work camp so his brother could get out. "He knew what was waiting for him." He feared he would be shot and was not used to the physical labor he would have to endure.

Chana found a solution. "She was an exceptional person. She got somebody with a wagon, [whom she] paid off, and they brought him home." Moshe had been in the camp for three weeks and "he became an old man." He had worked for ten hours a day "and they had soup for lunch. That's it."

"My father built a bunker [under a building] with another neighbor from across the street," which could hold ten people, in preparation for another action.

That action came on February 1, 1943, when German security police and Ukrainian auxiliaries surrounded Buczacz. Some Jews were shot trying to escape, another several hundred were murdered during the roundup, while up to 3,600—men and women of all ages, and children—were caught and held. The next morning, they were taken in groups to pits that had been dug by Ukrainian construction workers on Fedor Hill. Standing on the pit's lip, they were forced to throw their valuables into buckets and then shot.[11]

As the action began, the Hoffmans fled to the bunker. "My brother had typhus, so . . . they wouldn't take us into the bunker." But because Moshe built it, he forced the others to let his family in. Her brother stayed between their parents, while Bronia was next to them.

"We heard people on the path [outside]. We kept quiet and we heard the Germans smacking the walls and knocking the floors. Then it got quiet." The following day, calm had returned "and we all went back to our place."

"Within a couple of weeks we had to move again. We had to move to town" as the Germans forced the surviving Jews into smaller and smaller areas. The family moved into the cellar of a large, cold building at a cemetery. "We got a corner of a room and somebody else got another corner."

The family wasn't in the center of town yet, and it wasn't a sealed-off ghetto at this point.

The Germans and their Ukrainian allies struck again on April 13, 1943, in a three-day action during which about 600 Jews were shot during the roundup. Another 2,800 to 3,000 Jews, most of whom were in hiding, were taken to Fedor Hill where some of the

Ukrainians tore gold teeth out of the mouths of their still-living victims and wedding rings from fingers. Then, the Germans and Ukrainians shot them all.[12]

"My cousins, my uncles, my cousins died. . . . My uncle died, Mendel, and everybody." A bounty was put on Jews' heads. "Anybody could bring a Jew into the police and get a pound of sugar."

The last action came on June 26, 1943. By this time, the Germans had concentrated the remaining Jews they could find into a ghetto in Buczacz. About 100 Jews who were there were taken to the Jewish cemetery on Baszty Hill, about 300 yards north of the city, and shot.[13]

During the following weeks, the slaughter continued when Ukrainian policemen took the Jews they had captured to the cemetery where they murdered them. During the first half of July 1943, about 1,800 Jews who had been caught in the city and surrounding areas, including those in the Podhajecka labor camp, were taken to the cemetery where they were forced to strip before being murdered.[14]

"In the middle of the night, we heard shooting" during one of the sweeps. When the shooting stopped, "we started running" to get across the nearby Strypa River. "There was a little bridge and the machine gun was shooting. Some people were falling in front of us. Nobody could swim. I couldn't swim. My brother couldn't swim." But the river was shallow enough for her parents to wade across. "My father, we were in the middle, and my mother on each side. We were like lying flat and they dragged us."

On the other side, "we started running to houses where we used to live and the neighbors let us in, [hiding] on top of potatoes in the basement. . . . We stayed there the following day."

Then, the woman who had been their neighbor ordered them to leave. If caught, non-Jews who harbored Jews were frequently shot.

So the Hoffmans returned to the house at the cemetery. A few of the people who had been there before the sweep had returned as well.

"My mother says, 'It's no good. We have to get out of here. . . . It's not going to get any better."

Bronia's parents paid someone with jewelry to take them in.

The city was now officially *Judenfrei*—free of Jews.

"What happened then, the woman [who took them in] says, 'I can't keep you anymore. . . . They got a hold of somebody [who had taken Jews in] and shot them down. They found Jews in their place and I don't want you here anymore.'"

The family sought refuge in different towns and with farmers. When they found a person who would harbor them, Chana paid for their safety with "money, jewelry, whatever she could give."

But such safety was always tenuous.

Finally, the family was forced to split up when the people who were harboring them said they could not stay there any longer.

Chana's reply was, "'I'll tell you what, you keep my husband and my son because we cannot walk together, the four of us. I'm going to take the girl and we're going to go where I was born.'"

So mother and daughter started off at night for the farm where Chana had grown up. About four or five in the morning, they were stopped by a German SS officer and Ukrainian police.

To be out walking at that time of day was immediately suspicious. They had no identification papers—"If you lived there, you would have an ID that you are Ukrainian."—and they could not provide an address of where they lived. "We had nothing."

So the German and Ukrainians assumed they were Jews.

"They took her stuff from us and . . . the German says . . . he wants to kill us himself. He says, 'I'll take them. There's a river over there and I'll take them to the river, I'll shoot them, and throw them into the water.'"

Leaving Bronia with the Ukrainians, the SS officer led Chana through the fields toward the river. As they walked, Chana told the German she had been in Vienna during World War I and told him the address of where she stayed. The German stopped and told her that he was born on that street. He asked her if she had any money. She gave him the 10 American dollars she had, "which he could have taken anyway." The officer shot into the air and told her to go. Chana went into the wheat to hide and wait for her daughter.

When Bronia saw the officer coming back, she took off running. He caught her near where other children were. He took her back toward the river, "I hear my mother's voice . . . he shoots in the air, and he walks away and disappears, and we start running . . . further into the fields."

As they were hiding in the wheat, they heard the Ukrainians coming, "looking for the clothes from the bodies." When they didn't find any, they decided the SS officer had let them go and then left.

"We laid there until it got very dark."

When they resumed their journey, they stayed off the road, walking parallel to it.

"So we go there [to where her mother grew up]. We got into a barn, and there were horses and cows. We laid down there. We were tired and hungry."

In the morning, a man came in who recognized Chana. Her father, Berel Frankel, who had managed orchards, was well-known in the area. The man told the two that another man who lived across the road was looking for them. They were ready to go there, but the man told them to wait because if they left now "my son-in-law is going to catch you." It was the custom at the time, that when a daughter married, she and her husband moved in with her parents. Many houses had two rooms. The older couple would give the young couple the bedroom and they would sleep in the kitchen.

"At night, he came and took us over to his house." The man there started screaming at Chana that he had wasted a whole day looking for her. On the table were a pitcher of milk and bread. He told them he would talk to them the next day, and sent them up into the attic to eat and rest, sleeping on straw.

Neither Chana or Bronia had any idea who this Ukrainian was or what his connection to their family was. They found out the next morning when he came up into the attic.

Berel Frankel had managed apple and pear orchards for a rich Polish landowner. He started having problems with some of the local Ukrainian youth who would knock the fruit off the trees. His solution was to find the worst offenders and make them bosses, including the man who had just taken them in. He paid them to watch the orchards to protect the crops and told them to take what fruit they needed for their families. That solved that problem.

The Ukrainian told them Chana's father had shown him pictures of his children who were in the United States. One picture was of Bronia's uncle standing next to his convertible car. Her uncle was a plumber who worked in shops in New York, but the Ukrainian thought he owned a factory.

The Ukrainian "knows all about each sister and each brother that lives in America, and when the war be over, my mother's brother's going to come with a big airplane and take us all to America."

This photograph taken in the 1970s shows a street in the former Jewish ghetto in Buczacz, which was then in Poland. (Courtesy of Bonnie Kahane.)

"My mother says, 'Definitely.' . . . So that's exactly why he kept us. He kept us there for nine months." Once a day, he would bring them food.

By this time, the tide of the war had changed. The Soviets had destroyed the German Sixth Army in the battle for Stalingrad, which ended February 3, 1943. And while the Germans still possessed a potent fighting force, and were able to launch offensive operations, the Red Army was pushing the Wehrmacht back toward the west, and ultimate defeat, as the Americans and British drove Axis forces—Germans and Italians—out of North Africa, conquered Sicily, and landed in Italy in September 1943. They would land in Normandy on June 6, 1944, closing the ring around Germany.

For Bronia and her mother, all that mattered was staying alive. But their safety ended when the man's 19-year-old son discovered them. The teenager, who was a concentration camp guard, kept pigeons on his father's farm. The pigeons had the run of the farm. "The kid came to see the pigeons. The pigeons jumped up to the attic, it was open. . . . He grabbed a ladder and he went up, and he saw us . . . and in two seconds, everybody knew that we were there." It was a small village with a post office and a store for farmers, and not much else.

The man who had taken them in, told them, "You better get out." He suggested two places where they might find refuge, but those people would not let them in. So they went back to where they had been staying. He said, "'Alright, sleep today.' . . . Within a day he says to us, 'The police are coming to interview me with a German. They send them to come to see if I am keeping Jews.'"

"We thought, there's no place to go. He says go into the chimney and [his wife] was cooking." Russian stoves of the period could weigh two tons and were used for heating as well as cooking. Such stoves also were used for washing and could accommodate a grown man. "It was a little dark there . . . we stayed on the ledge. I found out the smoke went straight up. You don't get choked."

Bronia and her mother could hear the German and the Ukrainians talking about where the Jews were. The farmer's wife said nothing during this, just kept cooking.

When the German and the police officers left, Bronia and Chana came out. With nowhere else to go, the pair went back up into the attic. But they could not sit comfortably anymore. To keep from being seen, they had to lay flat on the floor and be covered with straw. "We were laying there for weeks at a time."

In the spring of 1944, the Red Army drove the Wehrmacht back through the area.

"My mother got a hold of somebody who brought my father and my brother, and it looked like everything was going to be OK."

But war is not a simple affair of one side driving the other side back. The Wehrmacht counterattacked, and "within a week the Germans came back. The Russians wouldn't take us on the train. They didn't know themselves where they were going."

The family found themselves surrounded by Germans. A Polish woman invited the four of them to stay with her, saying the Germans would be gone in a couple of days. So they went into the basement of her house, where they found another Jew hiding. "Within a day, she comes home, she says [the Germans] took over my house, and they're telling me to get out."

The man, "he must have been in his forties," with them in the basement told them there is a place across the street where they can hide. In the middle of the night, the five of them crossed the street and ended up in a barn. The horses there became skittish and started making noise when these strange people came in. The man picked up a broom and moved a board in the barn's ceiling, creating an opening into the attic. The man pulled himself up. Then Moshe lifted Bronia up and the man pulled her into the attic. By this time the horses were making so much noise that Moshe decided they had to leave. He told his daughter to stay in the attic, they would come back for her the next night. Bronia's parents took their eight-year-old son and fled into the forest to hide out. It was the Lesniczowska Forest where the Germans and their Ukrainian auxiliaries were killing Jews.

"That was the last time I saw them."

Besides Bronia and the man who had been hiding with them in the basement, a woman was in the barn's attic. She had false papers so she decided to go out. In an hour, she came back with the police and Germans who were yelling, "'*Raus*, *Raus*, we know you are up there with a girl!'

"The man started screaming, 'Don't shoot! I'm coming down!'

"When he says he's coming down . . . why am I going to go down? They're going to shoot us anyway." The fourteen-year-old looks for a way out. She manages to pull a board off the wall far enough out for her to squeeze through. "I jump down on top of wood. I was bleeding. I didn't even know it."

What she did know was the Germans were still looking for her. Bronia found herself behind the Germans and their prisoners, the man and the woman who had been with her, and another Jew. She watched as guns were pulled out. She knew she couldn't stay there but she had no place to go. "I went back into the barn and stood there for a second." That is when a German soldier noticed her, a private who was taking care of the horses in the barn. Through the din of the horses, he told her that he heard three shots. He told her the other three have been shot, "and he wanted to get started with me. . . . He says, 'You're not going any place.'" He looked around, and there was no place for her to go, so he told her he would be back.

An old mattress was against the barn's wall. "I went between the horses, under their feet and I went under that mattress. I was tiny. I laid down. I was laying there, it quieted down and I fell asleep. I woke up the following morning [around dawn]. . . . No horses, no nothing. I slept through a whole night and half a day. . . . No soldiers."

She went to the barn door, but it didn't open because iron beds had been put against it. "I gave one push, two pushes and all the beds fall backwards."

She was outside, but now what? She didn't have much time to make a decision, so Bronia headed into Buczacz. She saw a group

This is the Jewish cemetery in Buczacz. This photograph was taken in the 1970s. (Courtesy of Bonnie Kahane.)

of people, so she approached them and asked them to take her with them. A woman asked her what she was doing out so early in the morning and then the woman says she must be Jewish.

"I said, 'Yes. Maybe you could take me.' She says, 'No, I can't do that. I tell you what, if you go straight there's a place I heard that some Jews are hiding there.' I said, 'Where?' She said, 'Just keep walking on the same road, the main street will take you there.'"

Bronia headed down the street. Given how early it was in the morning, she didn't meet anyone. When she reached the building where the Jews were supposedly hiding, nobody was there. So she went inside and hid in the back, wondering what to do now. The need to eat made the decision for her.

"I'm hungry like anything. I haven't eaten in a long time. I was dizzy from being hungry and so I decided to go to nearby houses and ask for a piece of bread. Maybe they'll give me something."

At one house, she was given a piece of bread; at the second, the door was closed in her face. She went back to her hiding place with her piece of bread.

"Within a day or so, people started coming in by the hundreds. . . . I asked woman . . . 'Who are you?'" The woman told her the Germans were chasing all the people, mostly Ukrainians, out of their homes and farms so they could build defenses as the Red Army started pushing back into the area.

Bronia felt a little better because she could get lost in the crowd. Then, the woman asked her where her mother was. "She's on the other side," referring to what had become a large gathering.

In a day or two, the group, including Bronia, was told they were going to be put on a train and taken to Germany. "That's OK with me."

In April 1944, everyone was loaded into cattle cars. When people would ask her where her mother was, she would give what had become her standard reply: They had become separated and her mother was in a different car. She would say, when the train stopped, she would find her mother. Perhaps people suspected she was lying, perhaps they accepted her story, perhaps they were too preoccupied with their own problems to care. No matter the case, her story worked.

At one point, the train stopped by a river and the passengers were told they could get out to wash themselves if they wanted to. Bronia was among those who took advantage of the opportunity—only to have the train leave without them.

"Two hundred people are standing by the river. They're screaming they left their children on the train. I said, 'I left my mother on the train.' What am I going to say?"

The authorities took those left behind to a building to register. "I was standing at the side when they asked, 'Where's your mother?'

"'On the train.'

"'Where's your father?'

"'My father is in Germany working for the government.'"

Bronia was told another train would come soon so she could join her mother.

"A guy comes over to me. He says to me, 'Would you like to work for me? After the war, you will go back home. I have a kid. I have a cow. You'll come with me to the farm. My wife cannot take care of all the things that she [must do]. . . . You play with the kid. You take the cow for grazing.'"

The offer sounded good to the teenager. The clincher was when the man told her they had plenty of food.

She got a shock when she arrived at the farm. "The cow was three times as big as me. The child wanted me to keep holding him, he was heavier than I was." The family's main diet was potatoes, but she had enough to eat for the first time in a long time.

The family was poor. "He worked selling tickets in the train station. He couldn't make too much."

Bronia worked for the family until the cow and the child became too much for her. "There was a woman sitting there [in the pasture where the cattle grazed], and she says to me, 'I see you are having problems with that cow. It's a wild cow. Nobody wants to take care of it.'"

The Ukrainian woman invited the girl to come work for her. She lived with her daughter and son-in-law. "'We have plenty of food. My son-in-law's earning a good salary. We're doing very well, and you'll see, my cow is much smaller and she behaves.'"

Bronia liked the offer. So she went back to the man whom she was working for and told him she was quitting to go to work for this woman. He told her that was fine, that she would have enough food there. "He was smiling and I didn't know why. I was still a kid. I didn't understand it."

She found why when she entered the house. "I got sick to my stomach." They had a Singer sewing machine. "I had never seen a beauty like that." They had big closets—"full of all Jewish stuff, not from average Jews, from doctors, from lawyers, from people that were very wealthy." They had expensive furniture, taken from Jews.

The son-in-law, who was in his late twenties, was a Ukrainian auxiliary. When "this guy didn't have enough Jews to kill, he used to go after Polish settlers." Many Poles, who were a minority in the area, had fled the area in fear of their lives.

But Bronia was stuck. "I have no choice." The woman who hired her was alright. "She wasn't that cold to me at that time."

Bronia slept in the kitchen and started working in the fields, paying a price for her inexperience. When she helped harvest the wheat, she didn't know not to step on the stubble. "You're supposed to shove your feet [through it] otherwise you cut your feet. I cut my feet." Even with bleeding feet, she had to continue working in the field and milking the family's cow. "But I was quick to learn."

She was with that family for six months when the Red Army conquered the area, driving the Germans further west. The members of the family were confident the Germans would return.

"They hated the Russians."

By this time, the cuts on Bronia's feet had become infected. To this day, she has spots on her feet where the infection was. The woman who had hired her insisted that she get treatment and took her to a hospital in the nearby city of Berezhany.

"They gave one look at me . . . they pour alcohol or something on me. I was screaming." She was in the hospital for a month as she healed. In addition to the infected feet, she had contracted a blood infection and had boils on her legs. "A lot of people had [these infections] during the war."

"I didn't want to leave [the hospital] because I didn't want to go back to the other place. . . . The man that ran the hospital was Jewish." The Russians had put this doctor, who had survived the Holocaust, in charge.

Bronia wanted to talk to her fellow Jew but couldn't—she was afraid. "I heard people talking: 'You should see how many Jews came back; they want back their homes, and the Russian government is giving them back their homes. They are chasing our people out.'

"I have to keep quiet. . . . I couldn't trust anybody."

A Polish girl in the hospital told her not to go back to the farm, telling her, "You'll never get out." She invited her to stay with her in Berezhany until she got herself settled.

"I say, 'I'm not going here and I'm not going there. I want to go back home to see what's doing.'"

So in late fall of 1945—"It was already cold"—she got a bus ticket through the hospital to return to Buczacz. "I didn't find anyone from my whole family. They were all killed."

Bronia met a woman and asked if any Jews were left. The woman told the teenager about some Jews who had taken refuge in a building, keeping the doors locked for protection. Bronia went to the building and told them her story. "They let me in and right away."

They told her about a woman with a baby who was alone because her husband was in the Red Army. Bronia was told to help with the baby and the woman would give her food.

"I'm back again with a baby. I hate babies."

When the woman's husband, Mendel Reich, returned from the army, Bronia went with the couple to Krakow in western Poland. Reich made a living buying and selling currency on the black market. He had Bronia selling walnuts. "I ate up almost all the profit."

Reich also had her hold the cash from his transactions. He was dealing in U.S. dollars and French francs for people leaving the country since Polish money was worthless. The problem was currency trading was illegal, so if Bronia had been caught she could have been arrested. "I don't know what I would have done."

Eventually, she met a friend of her father named Underman, who was also selling on the black market. "He was a big man. He grabbed [Reich] by the back of the neck and told him, 'You better let her go. . . . Kids are going to school, there are organizations for these kids, you're not going to make a maid of Moshe Hoffman's daughter. . . . She has to make something of herself.'"

Bronia had gotten through the second grade but was never able to complete her education. What she learned, she learned by herself.

Reich denied he was holding her and said she could go.

A number of Jewish organizations, especially Zionist and Communist, were active in Poland, all trying to help Holocaust survivors, including children, and competing to win them for their various causes. The Zionist groups were reaching out to orphans and children who had been hidden with Polish families or in convents both to restore their Jewish identities and to recruit them to go to what was then called Palestine to help form the new country of Israel.[15]

Bronia ended up in one of the *kibbutzim* which had been established to house child survivors and train them for Israel.

There she met a boy who had been in Germany who told her he knew of a man there named Hoffman and thought he might be her father. Bronia went to Germany and found a woman who had married a man with a similar last name. Her husband wasn't Bronia's father, but she had known Chana. The woman also had a friend in South America who knew about a Buczacz organization that was looking for survivors. That woman wrote to a man in New York, Alfred Summer. Summer contacted Bronia's relatives in the Bronx. They started trying to reach her.

In the meantime, Bronia had returned to the *kibbutz*, where her mother's family finally reached her. She received a letter from her Uncle Leo Frankel urging her to come to America. "You have a big family here. They're waiting for you." She also heard from a sister of her mother, Dora Martin, who also urged her to come to the United States.

Bronia wanted to get out of Europe where she had no family. Her choices were the United States or Israel. After she wrote to him, Leo replied that if she would first come to the United States,

The building in the back of this photo was once the synagogue in Buczacz. This photograph was taken in the 1970s. (Courtesy of Bonnie Kahane.)

he would pay for her to go to Israel if that was what she wanted. She decided to go to America because she knew her mother would want her to be with her family.

So she started the process of coming to the United States. While she was in a transit camp in Germany waiting for permission to immigrate, she met two other young survivors, a brother and sister, Lester and Lola Kahane. Bronia met Lola while playing ping-pong with Lester, who was also seventeen, in the transit center. As it turned out, the siblings' uncle was Alfred Summer, the man in New York.

Since they were under eighteen years old and had family in New York, they were able to immigrate quickly.

When she arrived in New York on December 25, 1947, she and the other young survivors were taken to a children's drop-off center on Jackson Avenue in the Bronx. Children were either sent to live with relatives or put up for adoption.

Bronia, who was now going by Bonnie, went to live with her Uncle Leo in the Bronx. When she first arrived, Bonnie was dating a man eight years her senior. She was seventeen and he was twenty-five. "He was ready to get married; I wasn't. So I broke up."

Bonnie Hoffman had stayed in touch with Lola Kahane. "We danced a lot." That was one of the ways survivors dealt with what had happened to them, not just during the war, but after.

One day, she called Lola about going to a dance. She was going, and Bonnie asked her to wait for her—"I'm going to take the bus."—so they could go together. Then Lola said, "By the way, my brother's here." Bonnie went with Lester, who took her home after the dance.

"And that was it. That was the beginning."

Bonnie and Lester Kahane were married on December 4, 1949.

"We got married, we had $60 between us. . . . We have the December month [rent] paid for, and it's almost a whole month [before the next $55 rent payment is due] so we have nothing to worry about."

The couple had moved into a one-room, furnished apartment in Coney Island in Brooklyn.

Bonnie's Uncle Leo helped her move her belongings to the apartment from his home where she had been living since arriving in America.

"He sat down in a chair. He says, 'My God, this is where you're moving?' . . . He says, 'You're crazy.' I says, 'Well, what should we do? We have no money.' So he went home. He was very upset with me."

Lester "had no money, had no job. He had no profession. Nothing." He had first lived with relatives, sleeping on a couch. But after a month, things weren't working so he moved out. He rented a place and worked at what jobs he could find.

After the couple married, Lester was working in a furniture warehouse, moving inventory. Then, he met a man who was going into business making upholstered furniture. Lester offered to work for him Saturdays and Sundays for free, in exchange for being taught how to do upholstery.

His next move was making furniture. Lester walked by a Coney Island business that was selling tables and chairs. He offered to work for the company—for $60 a week. The owner he was talking to told him no, he already had a guy making furniture who was being paid $39. Lester offered to do a free try out. He offered to come in on a Sunday and work for free for a couple of hours.

With the three brothers who owned the store watching, Lester "started knocking off stuff. . . . He was very fast and very good at it, and they said come in Monday. So that's how he started working for them."

He worked there for a while and then went into business for himself with a partner. Lester made tables and chairs, while his partner upholstered couches. "A policeman was our delivery guy" who worked for them off duty.

"Between the two of them, they could have made a beautiful living."

There was one problem: the partner kept trading furniture for sex. The officer who worked for them warned Lester about his partner that he was having affairs with women who had husbands and boyfriends, and that would get him killed one day.

Lester walked away from that business and started over again.

While this was going on, their two children were born. While Bonnie was pregnant with their first child, Lester got his draft notice. The Korean Conflict was going on, but because Bonnie was a Holocaust survivor and had no immediate family except for her husband, Lester received a temporary deferment. Their son was born May 7, 1951. Their second son was born April 13, 1957. And Lester never received another draft notice.

Bonnie did some work sewing to help with the family's finances. Lester found a job, a two-hour commute away. The couple weren't rich, but they managed. "We struggled dollar to dollar. That is how we all, all of us in a way, we did the same thing. Very few of us walked away making big money."

Lester died on August 27, 2017. Bonnie now lives in Florida. One son spent a career as a dentist, while the other retired after a career making film trailers for movies in Hollywood.

Bonnie credits her survival to her mother, who was a strong, resourceful woman who kept the family together and alive for as long as she was able. Bonnie said her mother might have been able to survive the war—except she would not abandon her young son.

Looking back on how the Holocaust impacted her, Bonnie said, "I'm not religious. I'm traditional for my parents. . . . They died just because they were Jews. That's it. They did nothing. . . . My brother, I still can't figure it out. My brother was eight years old. . . . They put him against the wall and shot him. For what? What did he do? He couldn't even sign his name. He never went to school.

"How could anyone have feelings about God with what was going on? Where was He when we needed Him?"

NOTES

1. Yad Vashem.
2. Yad Vashem.
3. Simon Wiesenthal Center Museum of Tolerance.
4. David J. Hogan, *The Holocaust Chronicle*, 150.
5. Yad Vashem.
6. Yad Vashem.
7. Simon Wiesenthal Museum of Tolerance.
8. Yad Vashem.
9. Yad Vashem.
10. Yad Vashem.
11. Yad Vashem.
12. Yad Vashem.
13. Yad Vashem.
14. Yad Vashem.
15. Shimon Redlich, *Life in Transit: Jews in Post War Lodz 1945–1950* (n.p.: Academic Studies Press, 2010): 156–164.

"My revenge is my life. I have a son. I have two grandsons. This is my revenge."

—Ryszarda Rozenblum

CHAPTER 6

SURVIVAL AND DEATH IN LODZ

Ryszarda Rozenblum, formerly Ryszarda Einfeld

The city's name became Litzmannstadt in November 1939, shortly after the area which had been a part of Poland was incorporated into Nazi Germany.[1]

For Ryszarda Rozenblum, it will always be Lodz, the city where her family was locked into the first organized ghetto set up by the Nazi regime.[2] She was the only one of the six in her family to survive.

Ryszarda Einfeld was born January 15, 1929, in Lodz to Aaron and Cecila (Goldstein) Einfeld. She was the second of four children. Her brother, Jacob, was three years older, while her sister, Rivka, was three years younger, and her other sister, Fagela, was six years younger.

"I had a beautiful childhood, lovely parents. We laughed a lot. My [maternal] grandparents lived nearby. I went to two schools." Her main education was at a girls' school, Havet Zelav. A few afternoons each week she also went to Beit Yaakov to learn about Jewish life. "It's also for religious children."

"We weren't rich but we were very happy."

Ryszarda grew up in a religious Hasidic family. Her father was a Zionist and a member of Agudath Israel, an Orthodox Jewish political movement. Aaron's parents, a brother, and other relatives had emigrated to Palestine, which was then under British rule through a mandate from the League of Nations. The area had for centuries been under the rule of the Turks, who had ruled the Ottoman Empire until their defeat in World War I as an ally of Germany.[3]

Aaron worked as an accountant for a company in Lodz. The family lived in an apartment house along with other Jews, as well as Germans and Poles. The city, Poland's second largest, was the country's major textile center, an industry which employed many Jews. The population was about 665,000, of which approximately 233,000 were Jews and 66,500 were Germans.[4]

Aaron Einfeld taught his children to be kind to others. "Always my father [taught us] . . . even a child [can] always help and be kind. This was my upbringing in my house in Lodz. He loved people, he loved everybody. I love people, this is true, because I know there is good."

"My mother was very busy with four children, my father, too."

The Germans and Poles who lived in the apartment building "were nice to us and said, 'Hello.'"

Living in this cultural mix, Ryszarda spoke Yiddish and Polish, and could understand German but did not speak it.

"I did not have trouble with the Poles and Germans. . . . I was a child . . . I was with everybody, Polish, German children, we played together."

Her father had to deal with anti-Semitism occasionally. Aaron wore traditional Hasidic clothes which marked him as a Jew. "My father once came home and said on the street . . . someone approached him in a not nice way and so later police came."

Aaron and Cecila raised their children not to respond to nasty things which might be said to them by others. "This is the way we were brought up to be kind, to be nice to people."

The Einfelds also emphasized education for their children. "My father was thinking, when I finish school . . . I could go become a teacher in Krakow."

Ryszarda and her siblings were among the more fortunate children in pre-war Poland.

Ryszarda Rozenblum says Kaddish, the prayer for the dead, during her visit in 1953 to the site of the death camp at Chelmno where her family was murdered in 1942. (Courtesy of Ryszarda Rozemblum.)

During the Great Depression in the 1930s, the Polish government worked to exclude Jews from the economy. Jewish workers normally could find employment only with other Jews, but Poland had few Jewish industrialists. As unemployment grew, most Jewish workers were left out of the welfare system because of the way it was organized. Jews also were increasingly squeezed out of professions, and in 1938, they were excluded from the legal system. The government also restricted the number of Jews who were admitted into secondary schools and did not fund Jewish schools, as required by the Treaty of Versailles which formally ended World War I.[5] In the early 1930s, one-third of Polish Jews—about 1 million people—were living in poverty. Jewish children throughout the country were suffering from malnutrition and living in impoverished neighborhoods. In Lodz, 73 percent of the Jewish children lived with their families in a single room which usually lacked bathrooms. Many Jewish children survived through the help of Jewish organizations, such as the American Jewish Joint Distribution Committee. Even with this help, many Jewish children were in poor health and could not attend school because they did not have the shoes and clothing they needed.[6]

Then, things got worse.

Ryszarda's world was shattered on September 8, 1939, when troops of the German Army, the Wehrmacht, captured Lodz.[7] The invasion had started a week before, on September 1, as Nazi Fuhrer Adolf Hitler launched the next phase of his quest for Lebensraum, or living space, for the German people. Britain and France had entered the war on September 3 after an ultimatum demanding Germany withdraw from Poland expired.

"When the Germans came . . . all of a sudden I saw children . . . my friends, the German children, going with flowers to the German soldiers, and they were so happy, they were greeting them. So I said to my mom, 'The children are so happy, they are going with flowers, they are smiling, they are so happy.' She started to cry. She said, 'Not for us. Not for us.'"

By September 17, Poland had essentially been crushed. What remained of the Polish army was cut off and surrounded, doomed to eventual defeat, except for a small number of troops on the Soviet border.[8]

On that morning, Soviet Red Army troops crossed the border into eastern Poland, using the excuse that Poland was already a dead state, making the Soviet-Polish non-aggression treaty a dead document.[9] In reality, a non-aggression treaty between Germany and the Soviet Union had been signed on August 23, 1939.[10] The treaty was vital for Germany if it was to start the invasion on September 1 because Hitler needed to keep the Red Army neutral. The treaty also included a secret agreement for the division of Poland between the two dictatorships.

When the fighting was over, Poland was dissected into three parts. The eastern portion was occupied by the Soviet Union. The western and central portions were under Nazi control. Much of western Poland was incorporated into Germany proper, while central Poland became the General Government.[11] Poland had been erased from the map.

Much of the area that was made part of the Third Reich had been part of Germany before World War I. Under an October 8, 1939, decree issued by Reichsführer Heinrich Himmler, those provinces which had become part of Poland in 1918 were again brought into Germany. This eliminated the Polish corridor which had separated East Prussia from the rest of Germany created to provide an otherwise land-locked Poland with access to the Baltic Sea. The Polish province of Lodz was also made part of Germany.[12]

The Nazi plan was to bring an estimated 175,000 ethnic Germans from further east to the newly incorporated areas, to eventually be followed by another 135,000. To make room for them, Poles and Jews were to be expelled under a decree Himmler issued October 10, 1939. Approximately 650,000 Jews lived in those areas. On September 10, Himmler had ordered 550,000 Jews to be forced into the General Government zone, bringing the Jewish population there to about two million. Some 1.5 million Polish peasants were also to be driven from their homes into the General Government zone, along with Polish intellectuals and any Pole suspected of being anti-German.[13] While that was the goal, the General Government area was hard-pressed to absorb that many people, meaning deportations were stretched over 1939 and 1940.[14]

The Germans renamed Lodz as Litzmannstadt after the Imperial German Army General Karl Litzmann who commanded the troops which had captured the city in World War I.[15] Litzmann had become a member of the Nazi party.

Starting September 18, 1939, the Germans took over all major Jewish businesses in Lodz. Jews had to wear a yellow Star of David when they left their homes, Jewish shops had to be open on Jewish holidays and had to be marked as Jewish owned. Synagogue services were prohibited.

Jews could not own cars or radios, and could not use public transportation. They could not leave the city without special permission. An order issued in October banned non-Jews from buying or leasing Jewish-owned businesses without a special permit. In November, an order blocked Jewish bank accounts, limiting withdrawals to 250 zlotys (about $5 to $10) a week. Families were only allowed to have less than $100 in cash.[16]

Germans, with the help of some Poles, looted Jewish stores and homes. At times, an entire house and its contents would be stolen, while in other cases, only furniture and valuables were taken. When caught on the streets, Jewish men and women were forced to do such things as haul heavy loads, work in military buildings, and clear streets of debris left from the fighting.[17]

On February 8, 1940, a formal ghetto was established in two of Lodz's poorest areas. More than 160,000 Jews were crammed into 31,721 apartments, most of which had only one room. Only 725 had running water. Electricity could not be used between 8

Ryszarda Rozenblum, center of the back row, was with a group during the 1953 dedication of the memorial to the children who were murdered at the Lodz ghetto during the Holocaust. (Courtesy of Ryszarda Rozenblum.)

P.M. and 6 A.M. The ghetto was enclosed on May 1 with barbed wire. German police were ordered to shoot any Jew who approached the fence. No warning would be given.[18]

But the evictions had started even before the ghetto was officially established. "They threw us out of our apartment. You could only take what you could handle. You know, leave everything. So we left. . . . This was in an afternoon in December. It was cold and we were walking, walking far. So we finally came to the place. They gave us one room, one room for all of us."

Her father was an intellectual who had brought a few books with him and pushed education. Jacob and Ryszarda started going to school in the ghetto.

In October 1939, when the ghetto was being organized, the Germans ordered a Judenrat, or Jewish Council, to be formed to serve as a kind of government. The Nazis choose Mordechai Chaim Rumkowski, the manager of a Jewish orphanage, as its president. He was ordered to pick the twenty-one members of the council, whom the Germans then imprisoned as hostages. After he was beaten by the Germans when he tried to have them freed, Rumkowski was ordered to name a new council, which he had trouble doing but finally accomplished.[19]

Rumkowski was responsible, along with the council, for carrying out German demands for money and valuables, for providing workers for forced labor, and for organizing deportations. To help him run the ghetto, he had 400 Jewish police officers and three jails.[20] Accused of acting regally, Rumkowski issued money with his portrait and signature on it, and stamps with his picture, as well as starting a postal service.[21] He has been credited with working to save Jewish lives, while also being accused of acting as dictator over the ghetto, doing the Nazis' will.

In an attempt to save lives, Rumkowski had gotten the Germans to agree to his setting up of workshops which would produce products for Germany's war effort and civilian market. By July 1941, about 40,000 of the ghetto's 160,000 Jews were making textiles and equipment for the Germans.[22] He also received German permission to open schools which taught in Yiddish and Hebrew, enrolling 5,000 children.[23]

Deportations began in January 1942, with young children and the elderly—those whom the Germans considered unproductive—being targeted.[24]

"The Germans said the children . . . are the future of a nation. The principle was to get rid of the children."

To save as many children as possible, Rumkowski had children as young as ten years old working in the ghetto's factories and workshops and ordered ten percent of jobs to be filled by children.[25]

"He went to the Germans and . . . you know he made . . . a work camp for children, so they'll be working, so let's not take them away. So that's what happened to my brother and me. We could go because we were at the right age. But my small two sisters had to stay with the parents."

"There were over a thousand children," who were housed in buildings with fifty each. Boys and girls were housed separately. Each group had a teacher and an assistant teacher.

In Ryszarda's group, the assistant teacher was a Zionist, who taught them songs. "The first of all to sing, she was teaching us the 'Hatikvah' ('The Hope,' which today is Israel's national anthem). We had to sing every day the 'Hatikvah'" before going to school. To keep the Germans from hearing the song, she had the children sing it quietly while standing at attention. Some of the children had lost their parents, and the assistant teacher was trying to give them and the other children hope.

"They were teaching us that one day we [would] go to Israel." And one day a week, Ryszarda's parents would visit her and her brother.

Ryszarda worked in a factory which made overshoes for German soldiers facing the severe cold on the Eastern Front against the Soviet Union. She and other children made braids from straw which were then sewn into overshoes. That work earned each some soup and about nine ounces of bread a day. Food had become scarce after the ghetto was closed and Jews were no longer allowed to do business with the outside world. More than 200,000 Jews had been squeezed into the ghetto. Starvation was common, and when added to the unsanitary living conditions which led to epidemics of typhus and other diseases, and the lack of protection from the cold of winter, the mortality rate was high, accounting for about 43,500 deaths, twenty-one percent of the ghetto population.[26]

In August 1942, Aaron and Cecila Einfeld came to visit Ryszarda for the last time. They told their thirteen-year-old daughter they were being sent to a small town in the east, where the Germans said there would be food. Aaron was being deported because, as an accountant, the Germans did not consider him to be productive.

"I started to cry. I wanted to stay with my father."

Aaron wanted to take all four of his children with him to keep his family together. But a close friend of his, a rabbi, told him to leave Ryszarda and Jacob until he knew where they were going.

On August 18, 1942, Aaron and Cecila, along with their two younger daughters, Rivka and Fagela, left in cattle cars with other Jews. Their journey took them about fifty miles north, not to a town, but to the Chelmno death camp, which had begun operations on December 7, 1941. Between January 16 and June 1942, the Germans recorded the shipment of 55,145 Jews to Chelmno from Lodz alone.[27]

Three gas vans were used to murder mainly Jews, but also others, such as many of the approximately 5,000 Gypsies who had been held in the Lodz ghetto. Groups of fifty to seventy victims were forced to strip and driven into the vans' freight compartments, which were then sealed and carbon monoxide was pumped in. It took about ten minutes for them to die. The trucks were then driven into a nearby forest where a group of forty to fifty

During a visit in 1953, Ryszarda Rozenblum stands before the ruins of the building where her family and other victims were forced to disrobe before being taken to the gas chambers in the Chelmno death camp. (Courtesy of Ryszarda Rozenblum.)

Jewish slave laborers dumped the bodies into mass graves they had dug. Later the bodies were burned instead of buried.[28]

The Einfelds' murders were part of the Nazi program to empty the ghetto of most of its Jews.

The reprieve for the children who were still in the ghetto ended in September when it was announced that children and the elderly would be evacuated.[29]

The thousand children in the work camp were put into a large building. The children were promised they would be taken to a place where they would have food. Their teachers "told us to say, if you're thirteen or twelve, to say you're a little bit older" because Rumkowski had told the Germans "the youngest was thirteen. . . . 'Just don't say less . . . even if you look like ten because you are undernourished.' . . . We children, we had the feeling that something was wrong. We started to cry. 'God,' we said, 'where are you?'

"My brother was three years older and I was thirteen. I hit on an idea . . . let's run because the cemetery is not far [and we could hide there]. I was ready to run away but the Germans surrounded us and we couldn't leave."

To improve their chances of not being deported, "for the Germans, we make ourselves look better, older" by pinching their cheeks to make themselves look healthy.

Ryszarda and Jacob were walking together as the Germans took them out of the building. Suddenly her brother was taken in one direction and she was pushed in another. "I start to scream, 'He's my brother I will go with him, I will go with him.' . . . I didn't let go of his hand."

So the German guard let her stay with Jacob instead of getting onto the truck that would have taken her to her death in Chelmno.

She became one of only thirteen children who were not deported.

Because those children had no families, Rumkowski asked other Jewish families to adopt them. Ryszarda was adopted by Leo and Dena Lederman. Leo was a manager at the railroad, thus one of the last who would have to face deportation. Her brother was adopted by a different family.

After the massive deportations ended in September 1942, life in the ghetto returned to what passed as normal, with the surviving 77,000 Jews starving and working for the Germans, and Rumkowski overseeing life. For a year and a half, ghetto factories were filling orders for the Wehrmacht and the German civilian economy. Some Jews were optimistic about their chances for survival despite news the Germans were losing the war and retreating west in front of the Soviet Red Army. But others knew ghettos where Jews had been working in Poland had been liquidated as the Germans retreated, making them worry about their chances for survival.[30]

In the spring of 1944, Nazi ideology won over Nazi greed. The German officials had been debating liquidating the Lodz ghetto for more than a year. Nazi purists, such as Himmler, wanted to empty the ghetto. They were opposed by Hans Biebow, who was the head of the ghetto's German civil administration, and SS-Obergruppenfuhrer Arthur Greiser, the *Reichsstatthalter*, or head, of the Reichsgau of Warthegau, an administrative area which included Lodz. Both men were getting rich from the sale of consumer products, such as furniture, shoes, and gloves, to German department stores. Albert Speer, the Reich Minister of Armaments and War Production, also wanted to keep the ghetto open so the Jewish workers could keep feeding the German war effort.[31]

In the end, the ideology of murder triumphed. On August 21, 1944, the ghetto still held 61,174 starving, exhausted Jews. Almost all were gone by the night of September 5.[32] Beibow and Rumkowski urged the Jews to accept resettlement, with Beibow assuring them the goal was to save lives.[33]

They were sent to Auschwitz, where they went through the Nazi selection process. Some were sent to slave labor camps. The majority went to their deaths in the gas chambers,[34] including Rumkowski and his family.[35]

One of those sent to his death was Jacob Einfeld. "My brother, he perished in 1944 because his family that he was adopted by was sent to Auschwitz. . . . He never came back."

As Jacob was being taken to the train, Ryszarda wanted to stay with him. Leo Lederman stopped her. He was working at the station during their deportation. "I said, 'I want to be with my brother.' He started to cry and he said to me, 'I cannot save my parents. I cannot save my brother with his children, but you. Now please, don't go.' He didn't let me go with my brother. . . . I would have perished with him if I were to go."

Fifteen-year-old Ryszarda was among the 870 Jews the Germans kept in the ghetto to clean it because the deported Jews were not allowed to take anything with them.[36]

For those 870 Jews, it was a question of whether they would outlive the Third Reich. On June 22, 1944, the Red Army launched Operation Bagration which tore the heart out of the Wehrmacht's Army Group Center. The Soviets threw more than 2.3 million men equipped with 2,715 tanks, 1,355 assault guns, 10,563 heavy artillery guns, and 2,306 Katyusha rockets at the Germans. The Red Air Force had about 6,000 aircraft, including fighters, ground attack planes, and bombers, to put into the fight, vastly outnumbering the Luftwaffe along the point of attack. At this point in the war, the Red Army was also more mobile than the Wehrmacht, which depended largely on horse-drawn transportation. In contrast, the Red Army had received large numbers of 2.5-ton American trucks to augment the Soviet Union's own production.[37]

When the offensive ended in mid-August, the Red Army was on the Vistula River on the outskirts of Warsaw. The Wehrmacht had lost 350,000 men, including 31 generals. The losses included 160,000 taken prisoners—half of whom would die in captivity. The Nazis also lost hundreds of tanks and more than 1,300 artillery

Ryszarda Rozenblum working in her office at the Capital Knitting Mills about 1980, shortly before she retired. (Courtesy of Ryszarda Rozenblum.)

guns. The German Fourth Army alone lost 130,000 of its 165,000 men. During its 400-mile offensive, the Red Army lost 178,000 killed and missing and 587,000 wounded. It had lost 2,857 tanks and assault guns, and 2,447 artillery guns.[38]

While this was going on, Ryszarda and the others were cleaning out the ghetto houses of clothing, crystal, and other things of value which could easily be carried off. "The Germans were taking this away, of course. . . . We take out, make boxes, put them outside for the Germans."

At this point in the war, what the Germans didn't want was furniture.

The Red Army entered Lodz on January 15, 1945,[39] during its drive to Berlin. Those 870 Jews left in the ghetto survived by hiding.

The Jews had been housed in two large buildings, one for men and the other for women. "The Germans came again. [The Germans said,] this time all 800 people should be outside . . . [they said] we were getting food. . . . Everybody has to be out. Everybody. So two Jews went over to the German, 'What do you mean everybody has to be out? There are only 800 people.' And the German says, 'No more Jews.' The two people came back . . . [They say,] 'Run away because they're going to kill us. We knew that they were because we knew about the graves in the cemetery, eight [mass] graves for 100 each. So we knew that we would be killed."

Ryszarda was among about fifty people who fled to a building with a hidden room. A bookshelf with books piled on it was in front of the entrance. For two days, they hid in that room. No food. No fresh air.

"We were sick and I was coughing and everybody was tired . . . it was a very small room for fifty people."

On the second day, Poles were going through the abandoned houses. Ryszarda and the other Jews heard them on the street talking. The Jews started wondering if the Germans had left. "One of the people said, 'I'm going down and ask.' He went out and he said [to the Poles], 'What are you doing here?' [One Pole replied,] 'We have no more Germans. You don't know?' 'What do you mean no more Germans?' [the Jew replied.] 'No more Germans,' was the answer.'"

"We went out and saw some Germans running away. . . . I was liberated. We were waiting six hours until the Russians came. When they came . . . I was crying. . . . A Russian boy [who was 19 or 20 years old and was not a Jew] came over to me. He asked, 'Why are your crying?' I told him, 'You see, I cry because I see nobody. I'm alone.' And he started to cry.

"I was wearing a yellow star and he saw this and he said, 'I don't want to see that.' He cut it off with a knife. He said, 'We'll take revenge for you. Blood.'

"This is how I was liberated."

All 870 Jews—the remnant of the Lodz ghetto—survived to be liberated by the Red Army. Eventually, the city would again be part of Poland and officially regain its Polish name, Lodz.

Leo and Dena Lederman had also survived. "Right after [liberation], I was living with them . . . and I went to school."

When she was sixteen, she met the man who would become her husband, Mike Rozenblum, through friends. He was from Lodz before the war but had been in different places during the fighting.

"He was a very intelligent boy. He finished college after the war" in Lodz, earning a civil engineering degree. The couple married in 1946 when Ryszarda was seventeen and Mike was twenty-eight.

Ryszarda almost finished high school before their son was born in 1949 while they were in Poland.

This memorial to the murdered Jewish children stands on the grounds of their former living quarters in the Lodz ghetto. It depicts a broken heart with the figure of a child in the center. (Courtesy of Ryszarda Rozenblum.)

Before the war, Mike worked with his father in a tanning business, turning raw hides into leather. After the war, he had an office job.

Although the couple wanted to leave Poland, "we couldn't. There was a time that you couldn't leave."

Post-war Poland was a dangerous place for Jews. For months after the war, more than 350 Jews were murdered and a large number were injured in attacks by Poles. The most infamous pogrom happened in July 1946 in the small city of Kielce, which was

120 miles south of Warsaw. When an 8-year-old Polish boy went missing—he had gone to visit friends in a village nearby without telling his parents—his father claimed Jews had kidnapped his son, but he had escaped. A rumor then spread that Jews had kidnapped and murdered Christian children. An angry mob numbering about 1,000 attacked the Jews inside a building owned by the Jewish community. When it was over, 42 were dead, including children, and about 75 were injured. Police officers and soldiers just watched.[40]

In an effort to fight the anti-Semitism, Joseph Tenenbaum, president of the World Federation of Polish Jews, in June 1946, asked Cardinal August Hlond, head of the Polish Catholic Church, to help stop the attacks. Hlond refused, blaming Jews for the violence. He said it was in retaliation for the murder of Christians by the Jewish Communist-run Polish government.[41]

After liberation, Poland, with redrawn borders shifting its territory to the west, had from 30,000 to 50,000 Jews. Another estimated 40,000 Jews who had survived Nazi concentration camps in Germany and Austria returned to Poland, as did about 180,000 Polish Jews who had spent the war in the Soviet Union. The Polish government reported a Jewish population of 240,000 on July 1, 1946.[42]

At the same time as Jews were returning to Poland, they were also leaving. Not only did they face violence, but at least half could not find work. From July through October 1945, 40,000 to 50,000 Jews left. Between May and September 1946, more than 100,000 Jews left. In the two years from July 1944 to July 1946, between 266,000 and 281,000 Jews had been in Poland at some point in time. By mid-1947, approximately 90,000 were still there.[43]

Jews were stopped from leaving in 1950 when the government stopped issuing emigration permits to them, keeping in step with the Soviet Union's hostility to Israel.[44]

That policy was reversed in the mid-1950s with a change in the Communist government. Communist Party Secretary General Wladyslaw Gomulka, who reclaimed power, encouraged Jews who held onto their Jewish identity to leave Poland. Nearly 100,000 took him up on the offer, with most going to Israel.[45]

Ryszarda and Mike Rozenblum were among those heading to Israel, leaving in December 1956. They chose Israel "because Israel was taking everybody." Going to the United States required a five-year wait for visas.

In Israel, Mike went to work handling accounts for a leather factory. "He went back to leather because he could do that. He didn't know the language [Hebrew]."

As for Ryszarda, "I was stuck. I didn't have a profession." She found a job near where they lived in a factory that made sweaters. "I was crying and the boss came to me, 'Why are you crying?' I said, 'I tell you something because my father used to say 'I want you educated.' . . . I was very down."

After she was there for two years, the company built a new factory. Ryszarda moved to the office and was dealing with the public. "I had a very nice job. . . . They were happy with me. So I was there until I left Israel."

Ryszarda and Mike moved to the United States in late 1962. "I love Israel and I have a lot of friends there, close friends. They came ten years before me. Just my husband didn't feel good there . . . He couldn't work if he was there." The doctor told him his health was suffering because of Israel's climate. The only cure was to leave the country.

If it were not for her husband's health, Ryszarda would never have left. "I love Israel." And the only surviving members of her extended family were there, having emigrated from Poland before the war. Her Uncle Mordecai Einfeld and his family, including his nine children, were living in Israel. Her paternal grandparents were there as well. "They're nice people. All of them working people, not just Hasidim . . . some of them are teachers."

When Ryszarda, Mike, and their son arrived in New York, they stayed with a friend in the Bronx for two weeks. They then moved to Patterson, New Jersey. Mike was still working in the leather business, which he knew. "He didn't have such a good job. He was working. He was a good man. He was a nice man."

Ryszarda ended up working for a clothing manufacturer, Capital Knitting Mills, making sweaters.

The company "gave me a place in packaging, and I was a stock girl." She also was learning how to use the machines used in manufacturing. She later moved to the front office, working for a friend, Esther. When Esther became ill, Ryszarda accepted an offer to fill in for her, however, Ryszarda had insisted that when her friend returned she would reclaim her job. Esther never returned, dying from her illness.

"So it happened that I start working and they are happy with me. . . . I was different because I have ambition."

At one point the two men running the company were going to Atlantic City, New Jersey, for a knitting convention, and asked her to make a sample using a particular fabric. While she waited for that fabric to arrive, she decided to make the piece with another fabric. When the bosses saw it, "they said to me, 'This is the sample.' I said, 'This is nothing.'"

But her bosses took the sample to the convention. When they returned, the representative from another company they had shown it to liked it and wanted it put into production. "I was speechless."

Ryszarda rose to become a manager with 100 employees reporting to her. One of the managers she reported to had a habit of yelling at people in public. "He was an intelligent man. I listen to him. It is, like, I have chutzpah, I said to him . . . 'I'm a manager, a manager, if you have something, you call me [into] the office and tell me. Don't scream at people. You know what, when you scream, [the employee who was the target of his wrath] is going to the bathroom and she hides for an hour. You cannot get her out. Okay. So this is what I want from you.'

"He never came to scream [again]."

After 23.5 years with the company, Ryszarda and Mike moved to Florida because he wanted to go someplace warm. He died on March 18, 2009.

Looking back on her life, her tragedy, Ryszarda has questions for God, but still believes in Him.

"I want to ask when I call on God, 'How could they have murdered children?' . . . The men, when they took away the children, when I saw, when I cry, we said . . . 'God, we are here. We didn't do anything wrong.'"

After the Germans invaded, "I said to my mom . . . 'What did I do wrong? Why are they doing this to me? To us?' She didn't have an answer."

"I would come to this question of God: 'Why are we the Chosen People? For what?'" When she got married, "I have a picture of my wedding. I didn't have family. My husband has a second cousin. . . . We have nobody."

Despite what she went through—"in the morning and at night we get up with pain. . . . we're not eating"—she does not hate. "I love people. I love people to smile. I love people to joke."

Today, Ryszarda goes to talk to people about the Holocaust and her experiences, often in schools.

A group of survivors were honored after their presentation where they talked about the Holocaust with students. Ryszarda Rosenblum is third from the left. To her left is fellow survivors Genia Kutner and Gerald Beigel.

"I said, 'When I'm talking to you, it's not because I want you to be sad. . . . I'm talking to you so you know what hatred is, what hatred can do to people. For what? Only because we are different from you? Very bad. Just remember, you children, you are our future. You remember what happened and never forget what happened."

As for revenge, she is not interested in the bloody revenge the young Red Army soldier promised to exact for her.

"My revenge is my life. I have a son. I have two grandsons. This is my revenge. . . . [Hitler] wants to eliminate us, all of us. . . . 'No more Jews,' he said. He did not accomplish this. . . . This is our revenge. We have our families. We have children."

NOTES

1. Reitlinger, *The Final Solution*, 37, 57.
2. Yahil, *The Holocaust: The Fate*, 165.
3. Yad Vashem.
4. Yahil, *The Holocaust: The Fate*, 190.
5. Yahil, *The Holocaust: The Fate*, 190–191.
6. The Holocaust Encyclopedia.
7. Shirer, *The Rise and Fall*, 626.
8. Shirer, *The Rise and Fall*, 628.
9. Shirer, *The Rise and Fall*, 528.
10. Reitlinger, *The Final Solution*, 37.
11. Reitlinger, *The Final Solution*, 37.
12. Reitlinger, *The Final Solution*, 37.
13. Yahil, *The Holocaust: The Fate*, 138.
14. Yad Vashem.

15. Yad Vashem.
16. Yad Vashem.
17. Gilbert, *The Holocaust: A History*, 116.
18. Reitlinger, *The Final Solution*, 64.
19. Gilbert, *The Holocaust: A History*, 125.
20. Yahil, *The Holocaust: The Fate*, 210.
21. Reitlinger, *The Final Solution*, 57.
22. Gilbert, *The Holocaust: A History*, 151.
23. Yad Vashem.
24. Yad Vashem.
25. Yad Vashem.
26. Yahil, *The Holocaust: The Fate*, 323.
27. JewishGen.
28. Jewish Virtual Library.
29. Yad Vashem.
30. Yad Vashem.
31. Reitlinger, *The Final Solution*, 303.
32. Gilbert, *The Holocaust: A History*, 718.
33. Gilbert, *The Holocaust: A History, 718.*
34. Gilbert, *The Holocaust: A History*, 722.
35. Reitlinger, *The Final Solution*, 303.
36. HistoryNet, https://www.historynet.com.
37. HistoryNet.
38. Reitlinger, *The Final Solution*, 303.
39. Facing History and Ourselves, https://www.facinghistory.org.
40. Facing History and Ourselves.
41. The YIVO Encyclopedia of Jews in Eastern Europe, www.yivoencyclopedia.org.
42. The YIVO Encyclopedia.
43. The YIVO Encyclopedia.
44. The YIVO Encyclopedia.
45. The YIVO Encyclopedia.

"I can tell you, for a long, long time . . . I feel guilty all the time. I'm the only one alive. . . . Then I have my daughter, it starts to get better. But then, when I have my grandkids . . . I think God know why I stay alive—to have this family, these kids."

—Lia Volfson

CHAPTER 7

COLD, HUNGRY, LOST

Lia Volfson

Picture a little girl just two months short of three years old. She has strawberry blond hair and is wearing a dress. Her head is bloody. She is dirty and lost, wandering in the woods in the cold of January. Her desperate mother sent her fleeing from death, into an uncertain future.

That picture is of Lia Volfson. She was born Evelin Reznikova. In 1944 she was wandering around a forest in southern Ukraine, which was occupied by German and Romanian troops.

Virtually her entire family was wiped out during the Holocaust, a fact she only learned when she went to reclaim her history.

—

At 4 A.M. June 22, 1941, the German army, the Wehrmacht, launched Operation Barbarossa, its invasion of the Soviet Union, catching Soviet border guards and the Red Army unprepared.[1]

The Germans, soon joined by their Hungarian, Romanian, and Italian allies, attacked along a front more than 1,000 miles long extending from the Baltic Sea in the north to the Black Sea in the south. The Wehrmacht threw 3.4 million men in 138 divisions, equipped with 4,450 armored vehicles and 3,914 aircraft[2] in an offensive that German Fuhrer Adolf Hitler and his generals believed would be over before winter.

Facing the Germans in the western Soviet Union were about 3.3 million Red Army soldiers in 228 divisions, equipped with 15,470 armored vehicles and 10,775 aircraft of questionable quality.[3]

While the Wehrmacht was well led, the Red Army had been essentially decapitated during the 1930s when Soviet dictator Joseph Stalin launched purges of its leadership. The Soviet Union and Germany had signed a nonaggression pact in August 1939, which Stalin believed would prevent an invasion for a few years. The Soviet government also thought the German war with France would last much longer than the six weeks it took for the French to surrender. Caught unprepared, the Soviet forces along the border were destroyed or quickly pushed back hundreds of miles through Ukraine and Belarus. Romanian troops, fighting with their German allies, attacked the Odessa region in early August 1941.[4]

Evelin Reznikova had been born on March 1, 1941, in Voznesensk, a town about 88 miles north of Odessa on the north coast of the Black Sea.

The Romanians and the Germans expected to overrun the area and capture Odessa quickly but stubborn Red Army resistance and the Soviet Black Sea fleet's ability to bring in reinforcements and supplies stretched the fighting into October 1941 when the Soviet leadership decided to pull out of Odessa so the forces could be used in other areas. During the first two weeks of October 121,000 soldiers and civilians were evacuated by sea.[5]

Before Romanian and German troops entered Odessa on October 16, 1941, about half of the Jews managed to flee; 80,000 to 90,000 were trapped in the city and the surrounding area. Evelin's family was among those who were caught.[6]

During the initial occupation, the Romanian occupiers ordered Jews to wear a yellow star, murdered thousands of Jews, and looted their homes. Men were beaten and women raped. As the occupation went on, Jews were randomly arrested on the street and forced to either pay a ransom or be thrown into prison along with thousands of other Jews. There, they were stripped of their valuables and beaten, and women faced rape again. By early 1942, the Jews in the Odessa region had either been murdered or sent to ghettos near or in villages in the region. There, the Jews died, through murder, starvation, or disease.[7]

A few survived to be liberated by the Red Army when the Germans and their allies were driven from the region, reconquering Odessa on April 10, 1944. Soviet soldiers liberated the Voznesensk area about five days later.

Lia knew nothing of this history, her earliest history. Her memory starts when she was three-and-a-half years old after the area had been liberated. She grew up in Odessa as Lia Volfson, the daughter of economics professor Leeb Volfson and his wife, Chenna. Her parents discouraged her from exploring her past "because they don't want me to know that I'm not their kid."

But at the age of twenty-two, she pushed. "My mom said, look, she knows only that the city [Lia's birth family came from] was Voznesensk." So the young woman went to Voznesensk. There, she found a survivor of the ghetto her family had been in and non-Jewish neighbors. With their help; things she had been told by her great-grandmother and paternal uncle who survived; research, such as records from the orphanage where she was placed after liberation; and her few memories she was able to reclaim her history.

She discovered she born Evelin Resnikova on March 1, 1941, in Voznesensk, Ukraine, the youngest of three children to Leeb Reznikov and Lydia Reznikova. Her brother, Boris, was nine and her sister, Gayla, was five.

Her family was part of an extended Orthodox Jewish family with about 200 members. Her father had six brothers, all of whom were married and had a lot of children. They lived in ten houses clustered together. The family operated a mill; "they ground flour for . . . the whole neighborhood." If someone could not afford to have their grain ground, the family would do it anyway.

Most of the family was swept up by the German and Romanian troops and forced into one of the concentration camps which were built in the Odessa region.

"First they hang my father." Whether there was a reason or he was killed simply because he was a Jew, she doesn't know. Then, "my sister and brother become sick and they killed them. . . . And then my mom see what is going on . . . they're going to kill you."

In a desperate attempt to save her last child, Lydia Reznikova bribed a Romanian guard to look the other way as she put her daughter over the ghetto fence. In the little girl's pocket, she put a piece of paper with her name on it. Evelin hit her head going over the fence, probably on a rock, that opened a gash on the right side of her scalp. "To this day, I have a scar."

Her mother was later murdered. She was in her early-to-mid-thirties. Her father had been about the same age, perhaps two years older.

The little girl ran off into the forest, her destination, and future, uncertain. She doesn't know how long she wandered in the woods, but she was eventually found by a Soviet partisan, Dimitri Tshchak. "They have like a dugout. He took me there, he washed [me], he cleaned [me] up."

One of the things he cleaned was her dress. After it was washed, he found pieces of paper in a pocket. Putting them together revealed the name "Reznikov."

Tshchak "sees that I cannot be in forest and he took me to his family," who lived in a small village near Voznesensk.

He and his wife just added the little girl to their five children. "In the village, people don't ask [about her] because when we play outside . . . ten, twenty kids can be found, nobody count how many."

Evelin also blended in. She didn't know she was a Jew and "I don't look like a typical Jew. No dark, curly hair." Her thick hair was strawberry blonde. She spoke Ukrainian and not Yiddish.

And her name did not give her heritage away. "When he found 'Reznikov,' it's not a Jewish name . . . it's a Russian name."

But her age didn't keep her from playing a part in the war. She, along with the Tshchaks' children, smuggled notes to partisans. "One time I was [carrying notes], another time it was his son or his daughter, another time it was a different [child] because it can't come every day the same kid" so the Germans and Romanians would not become suspicious.

Evelin was a favorite because her thick hair made it easy to conceal the messages in her braids while she was taken on "foraging" trips into the forest.

After the Red Army reclaimed Odessa and the surrounding area in 1944, Tshchak took his little ward to the orphanage in Voznesensk, which was the nearest to his home. He didn't know where she came from or who her family was. He did leave a written record of everything he did know, including her family name, Reznikov.

Voznesensk Orphanage Number One was to be her home for the next three years.

The orphanage housed "maybe more than 200" children, with the girls in one wing and the boys in another. Most of them were six to eight years old, although some were babies.

—

When she first got there, Evelin was in a room with nine other girls when an outbreak of meningitis struck, killing a number of her roommates. "I took my stuff and I went. I said I don't want to be here. . . . Of course, police brought me back" when she was found wandering around in the cold.

She didn't have warm clothing, which was at a premium. "When we want to go, like in winter, go outside, we used one coat. You stayed ten minutes, come back." Then, it was another girl's turn to stay outside for 10 minutes. That coat was vital since the orphanage had no indoor plumbing. The children used an outhouse and washed in basins.

"The food was terrible." Whatever was available from local farms was brought to the orphanage. At one time, it was yellow peas. "They bring a lot of this. . . . In the morning it was peas, at night was peas, dinner was peas. For months. I cannot smell now these peas.

"One time they bring corn. They make puffy corn out of this, popcorn. After ten at night, each kid go to kitchen looking for this popcorn." Everyone was supposed to be in bed, and all lights were out, so the children snuck into the kitchen in the dark. Everyone was being as quiet as they could be "and nobody see each other. . . . Nobody got any popcorn because they got in each other's way." They all went back to bed, hungry.

But while the food was terrible, "the kids were very friendly to each other."

After about two years in the orphanage, her great-grandmother came looking for survivors of the family. Sarah—Lia does not remember her last name—was among more than one million Jews from the Soviet Union and areas under its control, such as eastern Poland, who were either evacuated or escaped on their own in 1941 and 1942 to the central Asian republics that were then part of the USSR, Uzbekistan, Kazakhstan, Kyrgyzstan, Tajikistan, and Turkmenistan.[8]

She did not find anyone until she reached the orphanage. "When they show her the name 'Reznikov,' she came to me and say, 'You look like your father.'"

And the five-year-old found out she was a Jew. "I don't know what does this mean, [to be] Jewish?"

While she was born to a family of Orthodox Jews, she was too young to remember. Since then, she had lived with non-Jews and in an orphanage operated by an atheist state.

Sarah took her great-granddaughter to her house. "It was mezuzah, it was Star of David, and then she start telling me what was before the war."

Her grandmother was in her nineties, too old to take care of a little girl. But an uncle and his family, which included two children, had survived, and he was willing to adopt her. His wife said no.

But it was through her aunt that Evelin learned her true birthday. Documents showed her being born April 20, 1941. But her aunt "told me that I was born one day after her baby was born, February 28."

Her great-grandmother was not about to leave her in the orphanage. Sarah found an older Jewish couple in Odessa who wanted to adopt a Jewish girl. Leeb and Chenna Volfson "managed to survive. They were in Tajikistan." But both their children, their two adult sons, died fighting in the Red Army.

"If something's going to happen again, war, whatever, then they didn't want more boys."

In 1947, Evelin Reznikova became Lia Volfson, the daughter of an economics professor at the Odessa National Marine Academy, and his wife.

When she met the couple, "first what I ask the man, 'You my daddy?' And he said, 'Yes.' . . . And I asked the woman, 'This is my daddy, who are you?' She said, 'I'm his wife.' She didn't say, 'I'm your mom.'"

"They were like grandparents. She was like forty-eight and he was fifty-five, and I was six years old. This is where I grow up, not in my mother's, father's house, in my grandparents' house." Her adoptive mother was sick much of the time, so Lia had to help her a lot. "In Russia . . . people at forty-five years, forty-six years, they were already old."

The war was more than two years in the past. Lia was living in a home in Odessa, an improvement over the orphanage, even with a mother who was old. She adored her father. "He was very good. When he passed away, three times I faint."

But now she had to deal with anti-Semitism. The murderous Germans and Romanians might be gone, but the anti-Semitism of the Ukrainians was still part of daily life. And Jews couldn't hide from it. Their internal documents carried their nationality: Jew.

When she graduated from high school, she had difficulty enrolling in college in the early 1960s.

Only a tiny percentage of the student body could be Jewish, which Lia discovered when she attempted to enroll in the Odessa State Agrarian University, where she wanted to study computers, economics, and bookkeeping.

The official in the registration office "said to me . . . only two percent can [be admitted as Jews]. What can we do with you?' I said, 'I don't know, but I have good grades, I have to go to college.' He said, 'Okay, you can study in the evening.'"

"I finished with good grades." She said she did not want to go to the university where her father taught because "somebody would think they took me because my father's here."

In 1960, Lia married Yemelyan Kilman, whom she met through mutual friends. The couple have one daughter, Larisa.

Only Jews who were retired could openly practice their faith. Younger Jews could only celebrate the major holidays, such as Rosh Hashanah, Yom Kippur, and Passover, quietly at home. "When you go to synagogue, if you are young, and they write down your name, and they send letter to your work or to school," and you were either fired or expelled.

Those names of younger Jews who came to services were recorded by rabbis "because the rabbi was Communist."

In the 1970s, anti-Semitism, which had never disappeared, was on the rise in the Soviet Union as record numbers of Jews were emigrating to Israel and the United States. Official anti-Zionist books and claims of harmful Jewish influences in ruling Soviet circles appeared in Moscow and other Russian cities. Some members of the Communist party and intellectuals worked quietly to increase traditional Russian anti-Semitism and drive Jews from the power and influence they may have held.[9]

The number of anti-Semitic books and criticism started growing following the Israeli victory in the 1967 Six Day War[10], in which Israel launched a pre-emptive strike against the Arab armies massing on its borders and increasingly threatening rhetoric to destroy Israel from Arab leaders, particularly those in Egypt and Syria.

Soviet officials labeled these books as "anti-Zionist," denying it was "anti-Semitic," yet Judaism as a religion was attacked and Soviet television was criticized for using heroes who looked Jewish. Zionists were accused of having ties to the CIA seeking to undermine Soviet power.

Official Soviet artist Mikhail Savitsky painted *Summer Theater*, showing a German soldier and a Jewish concentration camp trustee with a Star of David smiling over naked Russian dead.[11]

This increase in overt anti-Semitism was accompanied by higher barriers against Jewish students seeking admission to universities. Jewish parents said only a handful were admitted to the science and math programs at the prestigious Moscow State University, the strictest limits since the 1950s.[12]

All this made Jews fearful of losing the eased emigration policies introduced in the late 1960s under Soviet leader Leonid Brezhnev.[13] He had sought better relations with the United States and Western Europe, in part to bolster the USSR's stagnant economy and falling standard of living. One of the concessions the Soviets made was to allow some emigration of Jews.[14]

That increased emigration created problems for the Soviet government, both internally and externally. In 1979, Soviet authorities claimed some of the nation's most talented scientists, visual and performing artists, and writers were part of the 200,000 Jews who had emigrated in the ten years since 1969. Some of the Western-oriented, non-Jewish youth envied the Jews' ability to emigrate while they were still locked in by the USSR's otherwise closed borders.[15]

Then there were the Arab nations the Soviet Union was working with to make allies, who opposed Jewish immigration to Israel. Soviet officials tried to ensure a large number of the emigrating Jews would have to go to the United States.

Lia, her husband, their daughter, her mother, and her mother-in-law fled the Soviet Union in 1979, when 51,320 Jews got out—a record which would not be broken for another decade when Soviet President Mikhail Gorbachev eased emigration restrictions for everyone.[16] In 1979 and the following years, eighty percent of the Jews fleeing the Soviet Union opted to come to the United States instead of Israel.[17] Lia's father and father-in-law had died earlier.

Before they left, neighbors took over their house. When Lia asked officials for help, they refused. "No, it's winter; we cannot do this," she was told. She was told she was lucky she was not thrown out of her home.

Soviet authorities had taken the family's passports, which showed their citizenship, along with just about all other documents, "even that I finish college, [my] diploma."

"If you don't have a Russian passport, you are nothing. They can kill you or whatever they want."

Her departure was complicated by the fact that in 1972 the Soviet Union started charging a "diploma tax," requiring emigrating Jews to repay the government for the cost of their education.[18] Jews also were allowed to leave with only a small amount of money, forcing many to bring items they could later sell.

When Lia and the other four left, they flew from Odessa to Vienna, Austria. "In Vienna, they say who is going to Israel, who is going to go to America." She said her family was not given a choice—they had to go to the United States.

When Soviet emigration began to rise in 1972, all the Jews were flown to Vienna.[19] Israel and the Soviet Union did not have diplomatic relations, and there were no direct flights between the two countries. When they reached Vienna, the Jews were divided into two groups: Those going to Israel were flown out immediately. Those headed to the United States were sent to Italy.[20]

Italy became the destination because the Italian government was willing to help refugees and the Austrian government didn't want the Soviet emigrants to stay for more than a few weeks. The Rome area was chosen as the destination for these thousands of Jews because the American embassy there had a large staff from the U.S. Immigration Service.[21] The question of which country took the Jews became a point of debate between Israeli officials and American Jewish groups. Zionist proponents argued that all the Jews should go to Israel to help build that country, while American Jewish groups took the position that these were free people who should have the choice of where to settle. And American Jewish organizations were prepared to help Jews who chose the United States with financial and other support.[22]

Italy was not a particularly safe place in the late 1970s. Terrorist groups were launching attacks around the country.

Lia's train—they were told to keep windows closed, shades drawn as a security precaution—was headed for the Rome station, but she and the other Jews were taken off one stop north of the Italian capital because of the threat of terrorism. They were bused to a hotel in Rome, where they stayed for a month before going to Ostia, a port town near the Italian capital.

"In Italy, we wait for American decision."

Getting into the United States was just about assured. Of the 2,700 whose immigration applications were processed in June 1979, only five were rejected. But it took time for those applications to be processed. While they waited, the emigres were helped by Jewish and other relief agencies, such as the Hebrew Immigrant Aid Society, which also helped with housing and jobs in the United States.[23]

Life, however, was neither comfortable nor safe.

The town's post office became a gathering point for the Jewish emigres seeking news. It also became a terrorist target—a bomb killed three people and injured others. The apartments where Lia and other Jews were living were guarded by armed Italian police. "It was scary living like this."

In addition to terrorism, Ostia's Italian residents resented the flood of outsiders, who were putting a strain on such services as public transportation and creating a shortage of apartments, thus driving up rents. Graffiti started appearing around the city: "Get Russians out of Ostia," "We need our houses," and "Burn the Russian swarms."

In this atmosphere, Lia and her family were anxious to get on their way. "We went to Jewish organization to find out when we are going to go. [The woman she spoke to] say, 'No, I don't know yet.'" A problem was that an American sponsor for the family had not been found, which could take months.

"Three days later we have letter that we have to go."

This turn of events mystified Lia. She had expected an extended stay in Ostia, but they were only there for about ten days. She was not told who their sponsor was, or even if they had one. "If you have family, they are supposed to help you." Those without family were helped by Jewish organizations.

But Lia didn't turn down the visas she and her family received. They boarded a charter flight carrying about 200 Jews to JFK Airport in New York City. When they landed, they were taken to a hotel in Manhattan.

In New York, the family was helped by the New York Association for New Americans (NYANA), a Jewish organization which had been founded to help Holocaust survivors, and later expanded its mandate to help other Jewish immigrants. The organization provided help with housing, jobs, education, and health care, among other services.

Shortly after they had settled in the hotel, a man knocked on their door. When Lia answered, he asked her, "'What is your name?' I said, 'Kilman.' And he said, 'My name is Kilman.'" He questioned whether she was telling the truth. So she showed him her passport showing her name as Lia Kilman.

Radik Kilman, who had immigrated earlier, had sponsored his sister on her visa application to come to the United States. Her name was Lia Kilman. She was supposed to have been on that charter flight from Ostia.

Officials had confused the two Lia Kilmans. Instead of issuing one visa to Radik's sister, five visas were issued to the wrong Lia Kilman, along with her husband, daughter, mother, and mother-in-law.

That left Lia and her family in an odd position: no sponsor— until the NYANA came into the picture.

As for Radik's sister, that Lia Kilman finally reached New York three or four months later.

Now in New York, Lia and her family moved into an apartment after staying in the hotel for a month. She went to work as a bookkeeper for Associated Food Stores. Her husband received training in computers, and then held a series of jobs.

The couple divorced in 1985, and Lia went back to using her maiden name, Volfson. Her mother died about this time.

In 1991, Lia became an American citizen. She retired in the late 1990s after suffering a series of disabling panic attacks. "I couldn't work. Three or four times a day, ambulance comes because of me. . . . I work two or three months more, but I start making mistakes."

She sought psychiatric help, trying to find a cure. All she could find was an explanation: The panic disorder is rooted in her experiences as a child in the Holocaust.

Today she lives on disability in Central Florida, near her daughter, who has three children.

"I can tell you, for a long, long time . . . I feel guilty all the time. I'm the only one alive [of her biological family]. . . . I feel like I live not, not natural life because if my parents alive, my life going to be different. Of course, I was in orphanage; I was adopted. I feel like I live a different style of life. It's like not natural. This would bother me . . . with all my family killed."

That guilt eased eventually. "Then I have my daughter, it starts to get better. But then, when I have my grandkids . . . I think God know why I stay alive—to have this family, these kids. Now I have great-grandkid."

NOTES

1. Alan Clark, *Barbarossa: The Russian German Conflict, 1941–45* (n.p.:HarperCollins Publishers, 1965): 44.
2. www.operationbarbarossa.net.
3. www.operationbarbarossa.net.
4. World War II Database, https://ww2db.com.
5. World War II Database.
6. Yad Vashem.
7. Yad Vashem.
8. Jewish Gen.
9. Kevin Klose, *The Washington Post*, July 15, 1979.
10. Kevin Klose, *The Washington Post.*
11. Kevin Klose, *The Washington Post.*
12. Kevin Klose, *The Washington Post.*
13. Kevin Klose, *The Washington Post.*
14. *The New York Times*, November 11, 1982.
15. *The New York Times.*
16. Joel Brinkley, The New York Times, archives 1989.
17. Ari L. Godman, *The New York Times,* archives 1987.
18. My Jewish Learning.
19. Sari Gilbert, *The Washington Post*, August 3, 1979.
20. Sari Gilbert, *The Washington Post.*
21. Sari Gilbert, *The Washington Post.*
22. Steven Windmueller, "The 'Noshrim' War: Dropping Out," *A Second Exodus: The American Movement to Free Soviet Jews*, 1999.
23. Sari Gilbert, *The Washington Post.*

"I have a lot of questions. Why? Why did this happen to the Jewish people? But God is everything."

—Genia Kutner

CHAPTER 8

ON THE RUN

Genia Kutner, formerly Genia Kagan

Genia Kagan was born July 18, 1928, into a middle-class family in Pinsk, a city of about 30,000 Jews and 30,000 Poles, in what was then eastern Poland.

Her brother, Shaike, was born two years before her. Her baby brother, Aroni, was born in December 1938, less than a year before the outbreak of World War II.

Genia's father, Herschel Leb Kagan, was a kohen, a member of the traditional Jewish priestly family whose ancestors presided over the first and second Temples in Jerusalem. He also was a committed Zionist and a Stoliner Hasid, an Orthodox Jewish sect founded in the mid-18th century in Lithuania. The group later spread to Belarus, and their prayer house was founded in Karlin, a suburb of Pinsk, in 1762.[1]

Born in 1896 near Pinsk, Herschel was active in the Zionist organization Tomodachi Aniyim [Supporting the Poor]. While he was a Hasid, he did not have the traditional Orthodox appearance—he did not wear *payot* [sidelocks], a beard, or a *shtreimel* [a classic fur hat worn by many Hasidic men].

Genia's mother was born Miriam Friedman in 1904 in Rubella, another village not far from Pinsk.

When Genia's parents were born, Pinsk and the surrounding area were part of the Russian Empire. Following World War I, and the Russo-Polish War (1920-1921), the area became part of Poland, under the treaty signed in Riga, Latvia, on March 18, 1921, between Poland and Soviet Russia.[2] When they married in 1925, the couple settled in Rubella, a village with ten Jewish and thirty Polish families. Herschel made a living as a shoemaker.

The family moved to Pinsk when Genia was three years old. Herschel went to work at a lumber factory, Lurye. "They saw his potential. He was an intelligent guy, and little by little," he worked his way up to become the factory's director. "He bloomed in Pinsk."

Herschel's goal was to move to Palestine, the British mandate, part of which would one day become Israel. The rest would become what is today called the West Bank and Jordan. The British gained control of the area following World War I. The Western Allies, with the main effort led by the British, defeated the Turkish Empire, which had fought on Germany's side. The Empire was stripped of its territories outside of Turkey proper, with the Arab areas being divided between Britain and France by the League of Nations, a failed attempt at an international organization to keep the peace. While these areas did not become formal colonies, they were under the administrative control of either Britain or France, known as mandates.

To make the move, Herschel needed the formal approval of the British. While he waited for that to come, he sent his daughter, Genia, and her brother, Shaike, to a private school, Tarbut. "We learned everything in Hebrew, every subject, but a lot about Israel, preparing us to go to Israel."

The family never received the certificate they needed to move to Palestine.

While Jews had lived in the land of Israel for thousands of years, a wave of Orthodox Jews from eastern Europe, mainly Russia, began immigrating to the then-Turkish province in the 1880s, on what became known as the First Aliyah, a Hebrew word meaning "ascent."[3] A second wave, the Second Aliyah, brought more Eastern European Jews to the Turkish province of Palestine

This photograph of survivors was taken shortly after the end of World War II. (Courtesy of Genia Kutner.)

in the decade before World War I. These Jews were mostly secular, socialist, and idealistic. Mostly Zionists, they were fleeing pogroms and anti-Semitic oppression.[4]

During World War I, the British government issued the Balfour Declaration which promised to support the creation of a Jewish homeland in Israel. After the war, the British reneged on that promise to placate the Arabs, who opposed Jewish immigration and resorted to violence.[5] The British had also promised the Arabs an independent country to win their support during the war.

In 1929, in what became one of the most notorious pogroms, the members of the small, ancient Jewish community in Hebron, in what is today the West Bank, were attacked by their Arab neighbors. In the violence, which that lasted for three days, 67 Jews were murdered, and homes and synagogues were destroyed. The British evacuated 484 survivors, many of whom were saved by Arab families, to Jerusalem. Some Jews moved back to Hebron, but the British forced them to leave during the Arab Revolt in 1936.[6]

In Poland, life was good for Genia and her family in Pinsk during the 1930s. "We were middle class. . . . Most of the people were poor, you know, but I was middle class and that was enough for me. We had a beautiful home. I had beautiful friends from school. . . . The holidays were observed."

Genia and her brother would spend every summer before World War II with their maternal grandmother, Sara Friedman, in Rubella. In that small village, the Jewish and Polish children played together.

Pinsk was another story. "My mother did not have any Polish friends." Jews tended to live clustered together.

Pre-World War II Poland had freedom of speech and freedom of religion. "That's why we could go to Hebrew school. . . . The Polish schools were free . . . but anti-Semitic."

Going to either the Hebrew or more secular Jewish school in Pinsk, however, made those students targets. "In private school, you had to wear a uniform. It was a navy blue skirt and shirt, and it had a light blue decoration. That's the way [the Poles] knew that we belonged to the Talmud school." The students who attended the other Jewish school also wore navy blue clothes, but they had a green decoration on their shirts.

Genia had a three-block walk between her home and her school, a walk which would become a gauntlet of sorts when non-Jewish students threw stones at her.

Around Christmas time, "my parents had to close the shutters, otherwise stones would fly into our house, and there were a few killings." That experience has left an indelible mark on Genia, some eighty years later. "When it gets dark now [at her home in Central Florida] I close my shutters. . . . I have a feeling a stone will come flying in. It doesn't leave you."

After the war started, "when the Germans came, the anti-Semitism in Poland became much stronger."

German Fuhrer Adolf Hitler felt free to order the invasion of Poland after signing a non-aggression pact with the Soviet Union on August 23, 1939. The treaty included a secret provision providing for the partition of Poland between the two dictatorships.[7]

Germany invaded Poland on September 1, 1939. Britain and France declared war on Germany on September 3, and World War II was underway. On September 17, the Soviet Union invaded Poland from the east. Poland's brief period of independence following World War I with the breakup of the Austro-Hungarian Empire ended in blood.[8]

"Our half, the Russians took over. So for two years, until 1941, until Hitler broke his promise that he will keep the peace . . . we had the Russians."

The Soviets immediately closed the Tarbut school. Hebrew was banned. "I continued to go to school, but we did not learn Hebrew, we learned Yiddish."

"And life became harder. Lines for food . . . they confiscated every store . . . they confiscated the factory [where her father worked]. They told my father, 'We're bringing in a director from Moscow. The minute we bring our director, we will send you to Siberia.'"

The Soviets sent most of the rich Jews to Siberia but left Jewish workers and all the Poles alone.

The threat of deportation and separation from his family hung over Herschel's head for two years. But the Soviet director never arrived, and since Herschel spoke Russian, he kept his job running the factory.

Then on June 22, 1941, the German army, the Wehrmacht, launched Operation Barbarossa, the invasion of the Soviet Union. Hitler and the Nazis were bent on conquering the Soviet Union, to destroy Communism and to enslave the Slavic people, as well as exterminating Jews.

"We already heard what's going on in western Poland" to Jews under the Germans. After the invasion and partition, thousands of Jews had fled east to escape the Nazis. "The first thing they do, they kill the intelligentsia and supposedly we belong to the intelligentsia [a class of educated people who critique, guide, and lead in shaping the culture and politics of their society].

"So when the war broke out and the Germans were close by Pinsk, my father said to my mother, 'I'm running because I will be among the first ones [killed]. The rabbis, the engineers, the lawyers, they hang right away.' . . . My mother said, 'Wherever you're going, I'm going.'"

Herschel protested that he didn't know where he was going, only that he was headed east, into the Soviet Union. That didn't matter, Miriam was going with him, and they were taking their three children.

"He had guts to take his family . . . and go to Russia."

Fighting was beginning to reach them. "Bombardments are already started in Pinsk and we ran to the Russian border. I was eleven, my brother was thirteen, and my little brother was three years old."

"Half the city was running." During the three days it took to walk to the border, "we stopped at villages at night."

When they reached the border at Mikawitz, "to our good luck there were trains. People were running, many people had the guts to run but most of them were the young people. Fathers with children and wife were very little. We were the exception."

This picture of Genia Kutner was taken in 1948 while she was a member of the Israeli Defense Force during the 1948 War of Independence. (Courtesy of Genia Kutner.)

But being a family didn't mean special help. "We took care of ourselves. On the train, everybody was pushing himself. But my father was a strong man. He pushed up my mother, he pushed up the children."

The family squeezed into a cattle car which held eighty people, with no food and no place to sit down.

They rode the train 137 miles northeast to Minsk, where they had cousins they could stay with. The morning after they arrived, "the Russians are calling to us, 'All those who came from Poland, we want to take you deeper into Russia. Come out.' So we came out and they took us."

In reality, they took them back to Poland, back to Mikawitz. "They lied to us."

Herschel had a cousin in Mikawitz who worked in the lumber factory there. He took Herschel and his family into the house with his wife and ten children.

"Most of the people from Pinsk, from other towns, went back to Poland. They said Russia doesn't let us in, don't run. So that's why we have very few people saved from Pinsk.

"But my father said, 'No, I'm not going back to Pinsk. I'm waiting until the Russians will let us in.'"

The two families had little food. Six of the children would stand in line to get bread. "Only bread we could eat, bread, a little milk . . . so we didn't starve. This was important." The five of them slept on the floor since that was the only space available.

Herschel didn't wait for official approval to head east. The Soviets had decided to move the factory, and its workers, toward Moscow. His cousin told Herschel to come with him and his wife and children. Alongside this family of twelve, no one would notice another five people squeezed in among the workers. "Nobody checked, so we went back . . . the Russians let us in."

But Herschel's cousin had a warning: If the Russians "discover you, they will put you in jail. They are strict."

The family got off the train in Kiev, while the factory and its workers continued rolling east. By August 23, 1941, the Wehrmacht was beginning its attack in the Kiev region, a battle that would last until September 26, and result in the largest encirclement of troops in history when the Germans captured more than 660,000 Red Army soldiers.

But Herschel already had his family moving east again. "For the next two years, we were running deeper, deeper, and deeper into Russia" as the Germans drove deep into the Soviet Union. A week or so before the Germans captured a village, the family had already left.

Russian radio broadcasts provided warnings when the Germans were approaching an area, and while many Ukrainians initially welcomed them as liberators, many Jews fled.

"The Russians gave us trains, hundreds of trains." Thousands of Jews were fleeing coming from Romania, Bulgaria, and other areas of Europe. Russia was the only country to let them in.

As the trains headed east, they would stop periodically to let their passengers get out to relieve themselves, often in fields.

When they stopped in a village or city, the government provided hot water, but no food. What little they had to eat came from Russians who brought "us a potato, carrot. They didn't have for themselves what to eat. All the men were in the army. There was no one to work the fields. We were all starving. I myself am surprised" at their generosity.

Genia attributes their survival to "my father's wisdom. Now many people decided, 'I'm not running anymore, I have nowhere to run anymore.' They stayed in their villages and they got killed. . . . We ran until 1943 when the Germans were defeated in Stalingrad." On February 2, 1943, the Battle of Stalingrad ended with the destruction of the German Sixth Army, and the surrender of about 91,000 German soldiers. The Nazi tide began to recede after that.

But the trains continued rolling east, taking their passengers to Uzbekistan, Turkmenistan, and Tajikistan.

The Kagan family ended up in a barn on a collective farm in Margilan, Uzbekistan, with eight other families, all of them sleeping on straw mattresses and using old coats for blankets.

One of the young children had Whooping Cough, which spread among the children. "In those days they didn't give injections. . . . Only the older children survived."

Aroni, her young brother, died. "We buried him in a city named Margilan" in eastern Uzbekistan.

Herschel heard about a factory making silk parachutes about a mile and a half away in Fergana.

When he went there, he discovered many of the workers were Jewish refugees, most of whom did not speak Russian. Because he did speak Russian and had experience running a factory, he was made a manager.

He moved his wife and two surviving children to a barracks near the factory. The building had many rooms, each with two or three families living in them. Herschel managed to secure a room, the size of a small kitchen, for just his family. They lived there until after the war ended, two years later.

Genia finished high school. "When you are in Russia, you have to go to school until you're sixteen. Education is very important over there."

Her brother, Shaika, went to work in a bakery.

The family wasn't starving anymore. They each got a pound of bread a day, and her brother managed to bring some more from the bakery. And her father "knew how to finagle" to keep his family safe and get them through the hard times.

When Genia finished high school, "I had to go to work, otherwise you don't get your bread, your one pound of bread." She became a secretary for one of the managers at the silk factory since she knew Russian, having learned it when she was eleven to thirteen years old and then having spent another two years in a Russian school. And her father was a manager there.

Her new boss was Benjamin Kutner, a Jewish refugee from the Lodz ghetto in Poland. They would marry in 1949. While he was thirteen years older than Genia, "he decided to start up with me. I was sixteen years old. I was his secretary. That's how the romance started."

Benjamin was one of eleven children, seven of whom survived the war. Three of his siblings also fled to Russia and three survived after the Nazis created the Lodz ghetto. Another sister, Nadia Kutner, slipped out of the Warsaw ghetto, going from village to village being hidden by Poles until the war ended.

When the Wehrmacht reached Lodz at the start of the war, Benjamin's father told him to run to eastern Poland. Tens of thousands were running, going to such places as Pinsk and Bialystok, which is where Benjamin ended up.

But then he decided to return to Lodz. Many of those who fled returned because there was "no food, no work, they were young, and they left their parents, and they felt guilty."

Benjamin never made it back. The Soviets, who controlled the area where he had fled to eastern Poland in 1939, offered to send him and other Jews back. [War between the Germans and Soviets did not break out for nearly another two years.] The would-be returnees were duly loaded onto a train, and taken in the opposite direction, to Siberia.

The Soviets suspected these Jews of being spies for the Germans or having spies among them. They were held until 1943 when "[Soviet dictator Joseph] Stalin decided they were not spies." Benjamin and the others were told they were free to leave Siberia.

For Benjamin, that meant Uzbekistan and work as a manager in the silk factory since "weaving . . . was his profession." He didn't have a say in where he went; the Jewish refugees "went wherever the train took them. In Russia, it's not what you want, it's what the government wants."

World War II officially ended in Europe on May 7, 1945, with the German surrender to the Western Allies and the Soviet Union.

Herschel Kagan did not want to return to Pinsk because it was under Soviet control. So the family and Benjamin, who was now Genia's fiancé, went to Lodz. Thousands of Jews were going there. Survivors "came in from Russia, from the bunkers, from the partisans, from the concentration camps."

The family reached Lodz in November 1945, although the Soviets did not officially allow refugees to leave the Soviet Union until June 1946. "My father was so anxious to leave Russia that he bought tickets somehow. . . . He bribed, bought tickets."

The Kagans and Benjamin registered at the city's community center, which is how Benjamin discovered four of his sisters had survived when he found their names on the registry.

The Kagans had "no money, no home, no food. . . . Somehow we survived." As for Benjamin, he and his sisters rented an apartment in Lodz.

Then, two young men approached Genia's brother, Shaike, about going to Israel. Herschel said they would like to go, but they had no money. The Palestinians—before the Israeli declaration of independence, the Jews in Palestine were known as Palestinians—told Herschel not to worry. They would take him and his wife now on "Aliya Bet," or the illegal immigration to Palestine. Their children would follow three weeks later.

That three weeks stretched into three years as the British made immigration to Palestine more difficult in an attempt to placate Arab opposition despite the fact many Arabs had supported the Germans during the war.

The effort to smuggle Jews into the British Mandate of Palestine was called "Aliya Bet" because "aliya" is a term used to signify Jewish immigration to Israel, while "bet" is the first letter in the Hebrew word meaning "illegal."[9]

The British had begun restricting Jewish immigration into their Palestine Mandate in 1922 but became more restrictive as World War II approached. In 1939, the British government limited Jewish immigration to 10,000 a year, and then raised it to 1,500 a month, or 18,000 a year. Aliya Bet began in 1934 after Hitler and the Nazis rose to power in Germany. It continued during the war and after the war until Israel gained its independence in May 1948.[10]

From 1934 until the war broke out, 43 ships carried 15,000 Jews to the Mandate. The British turned two away and two

This is the ship Genia Kutner, her husband, brother and others sailed across the Mediterranean in their attempt to reach what was then Palestine. The 351 gross ton barkentine was carrying 794 passengers when it was intercepted by the HMS Venus. The British destroyer escorted the ship to Cyprus where the 416 men, 249 women and 129 children were interned. (Courtesy of Paul H. Silverstone Books and Publisher.)

sank. During the war, as Jews desperately sought to flee from the Germans, the British maintained their refusal to help these threatened people get out of Europe. The Aliya Bet effort managed to bring 15,000 more to the shores of Palestine, carried by 21 ships. But during that effort, five vessels sank, with 1,583 deaths.[11]

In the three years following the war, more than 70,000 Jews took part in Aliya Bet. Of the 66 voyages, two ships sank, causing the death of eight immigrants. In contrast, 10 Jews died during clashes with the British military.[12]

To stop this illegal immigration, the Royal Navy established a blockade of the Palestinian coast which stopped all but twelve ships which had a total of 2,108 Jews on board. The rest were interred in camps enclosed in barbed wire, with the majority being held in Cyprus. Other camps were located south of Haifa, and two had been set up in Germany. The most famous incident involved the SS Exodus and the approximately 4,500 Jews who were attempting to reach Palestine in 1947. The Royal Navy intercepted the ship and the Jews were returned to Germany, where they were held in camps. That incident gained worldwide attention and was a public relations disaster for the British. The British did release some of the Jews as part of the 1,500 monthly quota.[13]

The blockade was only part of Britain's efforts to stop the Jews from leaving Europe. In Poland, the British asked the Communist government to stop Jews from leaving the country and wanted the Catholic Church to denounce anti-Semitism so Jews would stay.[14] The end of the war did not bring safety to Jews, especially those in Eastern Europe. Pogroms were still launched against Jews and a number were murdered by Poles and others following Germany's defeat.

In addition to Poland, Britain made efforts to keep Jews from crossing the borders of Romania, Hungary, Bulgaria, and Yugoslavia in their attempt to escape Europe. The British also sought to keep Jews out of Italy, Greece, and France, and to prevent them from buying ships. The British kept a careful watch on all ship purchases. They went so far as to try to have the U.S. government cancel tax-free donations to Jewish campaigns on the grounds that the money went to help Jews reach Palestine.[15]

It was in this world that Genia, Benjamin, and Shaike would try to reach Palestine as part of Aliyah Bet.

After the elder Kagans left on their successful effort to reach Palestine, Genia and her brother were first in a kibbutz the Israelis set up in Lodz where there were fifty young men and women.

They had little food, but "we came with nothing . . . now we had a roof over our heads." And they all had beds, the young men in one section, the young women in another. "We ate together and we had already a leader and we talked about Israel, and we were singing and we were dancing the Hora (a traditional Jewish folk dance). We were getting ready to go to Israel, to go on the illegal aliyah."

But with the British watching, Aliyah Bet would not be easy.

After seven months in Lodz, the siblings, Benjamin, and other young Jews were moved to the Zeilsheim Displaced Person camp near Frankfurt, Germany, in the American occupation zone. In the aftermath of the war, ten million people had been cut adrift—Holocaust survivors, slave laborers, and refugees from Eastern Europe. The camps were established in Germany, Austria, and Italy to provide temporary shelter.

Genia and the others spent the next seven months there before heading to Italy in December 1946. The trip to and across the Alps would be done in closed trucks and occasionally at night on foot to avoid detection by the British. When they arrived, they were lodged in a large house in a town near Turin in northeast Italy.

"We were there for six months and then came our turn to go on the illegal aliya. So they came in trucks, in closed trucks," to take the refugees to the ship which was to take them east across the Mediterranean. The ship was manned by members of the *Palyam*, the naval branch of the *Palmach*, which in turn was part of the *Haganah*,[16] the Jewish self-defense force organized in Israel in the wake of Arab attacks and British inaction.

The move "was all done at night. We came to the ship in little boats." The ship was not moored in a harbor to keep it from being discovered by the British.

The ship they boarded was the SS *Kadima*, a 351-gross-ton, two-mast, wood barkentine that had been built in 1921.[17] They sailed from the Island of Palestrina just south of Venice on November 5, 1947.[18] On board the Italian flag vessel were 794 passengers.[19] About 160 of them were young children who had been born in DP camps.

"For four days, every one of us had . . . seasickness. It was horrible. We were on the bottom of the ship." A storm struck during one day of the 12-day voyage, making Genia and others fear the ship would sink. In their desperation, "we were saying, 'Oh, let the British come, let the British come, otherwise we are going to drown.'"

Their beds consisted of wooden shelves stacked up four deep from the deck. The passengers survived seasickness and the ship didn't sink.

But the British navy, in the form of a destroyer, HMS *Venus*, did arrive.[20] The *Kadima* had been spotted by a British scout plane on November 15, and the *Venus* intercepted the vessel soon after. The *Kadima* entered Haifa harbor under British escort on November 16. Because of the ship's poor condition and the children aboard, the Jews did not offer any resistance.[21]

The refugees were transferred to a cargo ship, the HMT *Runnymede Park*, for the trip to Cypress. They landed on November 17 and were interred in the Xylotymbou camp. "Over there, 20,000 of us already were there. They didn't have barracks for us so they put [us] in a tent. Imagine living in a tent, and the rain . . . Don't ask."

Genia shared a tent with her fiancé and her brother. When a storm hit, one of the men would hold down one side the tent, while the other held the other side with Genia holding the middle "so it wouldn't fly away."

While they had enough food in the camp, they were behind barbed wire. "Most of my friends were all survivors, you know, and all of them were in ghettos and in the concentration camps, and they were again" behind barbed wire.

There was education in the British camps, though. Six teachers came from Israel and were teaching Hebrew, history, the Bible, philosophy, and other subjects.

Genia was in the camp for a year, while Benjamin and Shaike were there for about a year and a half. The difference being that Genia looked younger than she was.

Golda Meir, one of the founders of Israel and its fourth prime minister, convinced the British to release children younger than sixteen and the elderly. The British would not release anyone who could serve in the military.

"My brother and my fiancé stayed, and I looked very skinny with two braids. I looked less than sixteen. I was eighteen. . . . When we came up to the British, the officers were sitting there and look at you."

If they thought a person was older than sixty or younger than sixteen that person was allowed to go. But young people who looked sixteen or older were turned back, regardless of their real ages.

"To my good luck, they saw me and they said, 'You look like a little girl, you're fourteen.'"

In November 1948, Genia was bound for Israel. A newborn nation that was already fighting for survival.

The British had decided to pull out as the mandatory power in Palestine. On November 29, 1947, the United Nations General Assembly approved a partition plan dividing Palestine between the Jews and the Arabs and leaving the religious sites around Jerusalem under international control. Arab leaders in Palestine rejected the plan. Fighting broke out when Arabs who were part of the Arab Liberation Army attacked Jewish cities and settlements. The main Jewish defense force, the *Haganah*, and two small radical groups, the *Irgun* and the *LEHI* (*Lohamei Herut Yisrael*), fought back.[22]

Israel declared its independence on May 14, 1948, the day the British pulled out of Palestine. The creation of Israel sparked an invasion by military forces from five Arab nations. The armies of

Egypt, Syria, Lebanon, and Iraq, with a Saudi Arabian contingent fighting under Egyptian command, attacked. The British-trained Jordanian forces also eventually invaded, taking areas which had been designated for the Arabs, east Jerusalem and what is known as the West Bank.[23] Jordan held those areas until the Six Day War in 1967.

With two breaks in the fighting through ceasefires brokered by the United Nations, the war finally ended in July 1949 when Israel signed an armistice agreement with its Arab opponents.[24]

When Genia reached Israel, she was immediately drafted into the army. Before she had to go on active duty, "they let me go to see my parents."

Since she was fluent in Hebrew—many of the new arrivals were not—she became a secretary for a logistics officer, a Sabra, the term for someone born in Israel. They worked out of a tent on a kibbutz, Mizra, not far from Afula in northern Israel.

"We were getting phone calls from different places in Israel, 'We need help, we need more people, we need more ammunition.' . . . My boss, the officer, he said, 'Genia, write down what they need and where they need it.'" She would record the information and pass it to the officer.

Genia served in the army until 1949. In the meantime, Benjamin and Shaike finally reached Israel. Shaike was immediately drafted into the army, where he met his wife. But Benjamin wasn't drafted because of his age.

On May 29, 1949, Genia Kagan and Benjamin Kutner were married, and eventually had two children, both of whom were born in Israel. Their son was born in 1951; their daughter, in 1955.

Because she knew Hebrew, Genia found a job as a secretary for a lawyer, while Benjamin opened a factory.

"It was very difficult to find jobs." The nation's population grew from 806,000 in 1948 to 1.17 million in 1949 to 1.37 million in 1950 with the arrival of Holocaust survivors and Jews driven out of their homes in Arab countries.[25] "There were people who lived in tents in the beginning, in 1948. . . . When I came, I went into the army so I didn't have to live in tents."

When Benjamin arrived and they married, they moved in with her parents, who had a one-room apartment, until they could find their own place.

"We were happy to have a roof over our heads."

Herschel had dreamed of coming to Israel for years before the war. He was helping to build a synagogue when Genia arrived. Her father died in 1956 when he was in his mid-fifties.

"A few years later, my mother met somebody from Canada. . . . and they fell in love. And he told her that he was also a survivor. He had a wife and two children" who died in the Holocaust. Like most of the men who fled as the Germans came, he had left his wife and children behind. "If my father would have left us, like all of them did, all of them or most of them . . . we would also be dead because in Pinsk almost nobody survived. So it's good my mother was . . . stubborn. . . . She would say, 'I'm going with you.' We wouldn't be here."

Miriam Kagan married the Canadian and moved to Nova Scotia, one of that country's Atlantic maritime provinces. After her mother had been in Canada for two months, "we started to get bombarded with letters . . . 'What did I do? Why did I leave my children, my grandchildren, my country? They speak English. I don't know a word. I don't understand anything.'"

Miriam wanted her family with her. "She started to miss me" and wanted her daughter closer to her. There wasn't a lot Genia and her brother could do. They were both married and both had two young children. Shaike stayed in Israel, but Genia did move closer.

"I wouldn't go to Canada, but my husband had three sisters already in America." Life had become difficult in Israel. Benjamin's factory had closed and he was without a job. So in December 1961, Genia and Benjamin Kutner, and their two children moved to New York City.

Neither had a job, and they were allowed to leave Israel with only ten dollars. "They didn't like us to leave. They were right because they needed people. There were wars, in the 1956 war, we were there, and then they had the 1967 . . . war, and then another war, and the war goes on after that. So they didn't like us to leave. They had difficulties."

Genia was able to find a job quickly. One of Benjamin's sisters told her of a secretary's job at a Solomon Schechter School, a Jewish school. "I came on Sunday. Monday, I applied for a job. Tuesday, I started to work and I stayed for thirty years."

Benjamin couldn't find a job until a friend found him one in his business in northern New Jersey. Since they had no car, that

Genia Kutner shows one of the awards she has received for her work in spreading the word about the Holocaust.

proved difficult for them. But then Benjamin's sister, Sala Shick, got him to join her in New York City as a diamond cutter in the jewelry business.

After Genia had worked as a secretary at the school for six years, making little money, "the principal said to me, 'Genia, go learn to become a Hebrew teacher. You'll make double the money you make now.' That's what I did. I went and asked my husband, 'Would you help me?' He said, 'By all means.' So he had a busy life, too."

The couple lived in Queens and, to become a Hebrew teacher, Genia enrolled in Seminar Herzliya in Manhattan. "I went for four years and I became a Hebrew teacher."

The couple moved to Florida in 1991 after their son moved there. Benjamin died in 2005.

Until recently, Genia had no interest in returning to Poland. "I went to Israel nineteen times, but I wouldn't go to Poland. But in 2015, I was in the synagogue and I saw an advertisement about the March of the Living [at Auschwitz Concentration Camp], and I was already 87, and I decided that I go. Something gave me a push to go to Poland. . . . I admire the Poles now that they let monuments [about the Holocaust] be built in every town. In the big towns, museums; in the villages, monuments with the names of the people. So I said to myself, 'It's a different Poland.'"

Then one of the American students on the march with her asked one of the Polish students who was with them how he felt about the monuments to the Holocaust victims. "And he said, 'We didn't kill the Jews. The Nazis killed the Jews.'

"This was his answer. It's not true. They helped the Germans kill Jews a lot. But there were a lot of Righteous Gentiles, too . . . and we're grateful to them. . . . But majority . . ."

Genia is still teaching, something she loves to do, only now it is as a volunteer at her synagogue, having touched the lives of about 300 people in the last seven to ten years. Today she is only teaching once a week. Over the years, she has been honored by many of the synagogues of which she has been a member for her contributions, and she has the plaques and awards to show for it.

Her connection to synagogues and her faith came from her father. "I was raised [as a religious Jew] ever since I was 3 years old. It is in me, in my heart. . . . My father . . . was building in Israel when we came, he was helping to build a synagogue. He was a *kohan* [a priest]. He was going to shul [synagogue]. He was going to help in the synagogue, and it is in me.

"I have a lot of questions. Why? Why did this happen to the Jewish people? But God is everything. I feel that when . . . things are good, I said, 'Oh God, thank you, God. Thank you, God.' I always say, '*Baruch HaShem* [praise God], *Baruch HaShem*,' whenever I talk to people. . . . I always say whenever things go bad, I say, 'God, please help me, please help me.' I feel somebody is looking over me, in my body. God is with me wherever I go. . . . I feel I have somebody and that's what keeps me going to the synagogue."

NOTES

1. The YIVO Encyclopedia of Jews in Eastern Europe, www.yivoencyclopedia.org.
2. Encyclopedia Britannica, https://www.britannica.com.
3. Berel Wein, *Triumph of Survival* (n.e. Shaar Press, 1990): 218.
4. Wein, *Triumph*, 258–259.
5. Wein, *Triumph*, 303.
6. Jewish Virtual Library.
7. Hogan, *The Holocaust Chronicle*, 1560.
8. Yad Vashem Aliya Bet.
9. Aliya Bet.
10. Aliya Bet.

11. Aliya Bet.
12. Aliya Bet.
13. Aliya Bet.
14. Aliya Bet.
15. Aliya Bet.
16. The Jewish Virtual Library.
17. Paul H. Silverstone Books & Publications, paulsilverstone.com.
18. Center for Israeli Education, https://israeled.org.
19. Paul H. Silverstone Books.
20. Paul H. Silverstone Books.
21. Center for Israeli Education.
22. Office of the Historian, United States Department of State, https://history.state.gov.
23. Office of the Historian.
24. My Jewish Learning.
25. Jewish Virtual Library.

"You have to understand that had I been arrested, I had no chance of survival. . . . There wouldn't have been anymore Henri Goodheim."

—HENRI GOODHEIM

CHAPTER 9

HIDING IN PLAIN SIGHT

Henri Goodheim

Life was good for young Henri Goodheim in Paris. The 6-year-old son of Jewish immigrants spent most of his time in Uncle Jules Ratz's restaurant, playing cards and other games with customers.

Henri was born in Paris on June 27, 1933, to Ber and Hannah Gudthajm, who had left their native Warsaw a year or two before the birth of their only child. Ber was born March 3, 1900, while Hannah was born August 1, 1908. The family's name was later Anglicized to Goodheim.

His parents left Poland around 1931 so his father could avoid service in the Polish army, where anti-Semitism was rampant. Later Ber would join the French army.

In Paris, the family lived in an apartment. His mother worked in a beauty salon and his father worked as a server in the Ratz, the restaurant owned by Henri's uncle, who had immigrated to France earlier. His father didn't speak any French, but since the restaurant catered to Poles, Russians, Czechoslovakians, and

Jews, that was not a major problem for a man who spoke Polish and Yiddish.

Henri spoke French as a child, learning from his cousins.

"I must say I had a good time during the summer. I was sent to the camp for children. And the last one that I went to was on the Riviera in France, which was nice for me because I'd never seen the sea and never seen . . . [a] palm tree."

"When I came back [from camp], I was only six years old, but something seemed funny. It was very quiet [in Paris]."

His world, and that of his family, came crashing down when the Germans invaded France, Belgium, and Holland about eight months after World War II started on September 1, 1939, with the German invasion of Poland. Warsaw fell on September 27. France and Britain had guaranteed Poland's borders, so after issuing ultimatums to Germany to withdraw, the two countries declared war on September 3.[1]

While Poland was being torn apart by the German armed forces from the west, and then the Soviet Union from the east, France and Britain mobilized but did not launch a serious attack on Germany in what became known as the "Phony War." The Germans called it the Sitzkrieg, the "Sitting War."

When the German army struck on May 10, 1940, France was defeated in six weeks during a two-stage assault which ended with the Nazi occupation of northern, much of central, and Atlantic-coastal France, as well as driving the British from the continent.[2]

Henri's father was called up to the French army and sent to southern France with other troops to guard against a possible Italian invasion. Although Italy was technically neutral for the first eight months of the war, French leaders did not trust that Il Duce, Benito Mussolini, would not attack. He had signed an alliance with the German Fuhrer, Adolf Hitler. They were right to be suspicious: Italy declared war on France and Britain on June 10, 1940, as it became clear France would be defeated.

As the Germans closed in on Paris, Henri and most of his family fled south. He and his father survived the war with the help of the mayor and others in a small town in southern France. Today, the 85-year-old divides his time between Brooklyn, New York, and Orlando, Florida. He has four children and six grandchildren.

After the war started, occasional air raid sirens in Paris sent Henri's family to the basement of their apartment building.

This is a star of David many Jews in war-time France were required to wear. Henri and his family were in hiding so they did not have to wear them.

When the all clear was sounded, they came up and "nothing really happened but it was an experience. I was just wondering why we had to run into the cellar." Life was changing for the young boy and he wasn't sure why. The bombing attacks in Paris by the Luftwaffe (the German air force) killed several hundred people during this time.

As the German army drove French forces back, tens of thousands of refugees fleeing the German advance flooded into the Paris area. Then on June 5, the Germans launched their final assault on the French army.[3] Paris, which had been declared an open city, fell to the Nazis on June 14.[4]

As the Nazis came nearer, Henri's uncle loaded his wife, and two daughters, twelve-year-old Suzanne and ten-year-old Josephine; Henri and his mother; "and a friend with another few" into an open-back van and headed south along with hundreds of thousands of other civilians who were fleeing before the German advance.

Three people could fit in the cab, so Henri, who was the youngest, sat there with his uncle and aunt, while his mother and the others rode in the open back.

They weren't sure where they were going—just away from the Nazis.

As Henri's family reached the outskirts of Paris, "more and more people were there. Everybody was running away from Paris. We had people on the bicycle, people walking, people with horse carriages, people with trucks and cars. But, of course, it was very slow progress because we can only go as fast as people walking, or if we were lucky, we could pass them."

Much of the journey was a blur for the boy. "The only thing I remember very well is that all of the sudden we had to jump out of the truck and hide in the bushes or under the tree or someplace" as Luftwaffe fighters strafed the road.

When they got back in the truck and started to drive again, "we saw [dead] people, [dead] horses just laying on the ground. You know, they tried to hide this from me, but I could still see some [dead] people there."

When night fell, they had traveled about ninety miles from Paris. They stopped at a farm, where the couple who lived there put them up for the night. "They knew we were running away from Paris."

The couple fed them and gave them milk. Henri, his mother, and his two cousins slept in a room in the house, while the others slept in the barn.

"In the morning we had to go on. They gave us bread; they gave us some milk. And we started going south not knowing exactly where we were going."

After another two hours on the road, they reached the village of Dun-Le-Poelier, population about 800, east of Tours—and they were running out of gasoline.

"So my uncle stopped at city hall and he talked to the mayor, and the mayor told him . . . you can forget about gas." Mayor Armand Mardon[5] said the little gasoline the village had was reserved for the police and the ambulance.

The mayor also warned his uncle not to return to Paris because "you don't know what's going to be." Mardon became a Gaullist resistance leader whom the Gestapo later arrested in June 1944.[6]

What the mayor did offer to do was to protect the family. Mardon told them, "You are Polish refugees. You are not Jewish, nobody will know that you are Jewish. You are Polish refugees; you speak Polish or speak whatever French you can."

"Only my uncle spoke French, and my cousins, the younger ones . . . but none of the older people spoke any good French . . . So I guess that's what they did. Of course, you know we were speaking Yiddish between us in the house, but making sure that nobody heard."

Mardon gave them a house, which consisted of two rooms, with no bathroom or running water. They lived there until liberation four years later. Water was brought from a fountain which was nearby and a little burner was used to cook food. Henri was washed in a big tub.

The mayor also provided the adults and teens with fake identity cards and ration cards, which were needed "to buy tobacco, to buy shoes, to buy a suit, to buy food. There were several categories. You had a card for the newborn, you had a card for the teenager, you had a card for the older people that went to work, and then for the elderly. So everyone had a different ration, different amount of butter, of bread."

Under the armistice which ended the fighting in 1940, the southern part of France was under a French government based in Vichy, which was subservient to the Germans.[7] The area, called Free France, was later occupied by the Germans in 1942, in violation of the original armistice. The Wehrmacht, the armed forces of Nazi Germany, moved in on November 10, following the Anglo-American invasion of North Africa on November 8, which was joined by Free French forces and the scuttling of the French fleet in Toulon by naval crews to keep it out of the hands of the Axis powers.[8]

Not everyone had fled Paris, including more than 100,000 Jews. The Germans recorded every Jew's address, occupation, and nationality, and confiscated their French identity cards. Jews were ordered to wear yellow Star of David armbands and subjected to a nighttime curfew. With the help of Parisian police, SS troops conducted periodic roundups. The Jews who were caught were shipped to a transit camp in Drancy, France, to await deportation.

In 1942, the Nazis caught 13,000 Jews. Among them were 4,000 children, many of whom were separated from their parents. After a week in the Drancy sports stadium, they were shoved into cattle cars and sent to Auschwitz Concentration Camp and their deaths.[9]

The armistice agreement, signed by Marshal Philippe Petain, who became the head of the French government on June 16,

1940, and his premier, Pierre Laval, included a provision requiring the French government to launch punitive measures against the Jews.[10]

In Dun-Le-Poëlier, the older members of Henri's family were able to find work. His cousin and uncle worked on a farm. "My father [after rejoining the family] worked in the woods, you know, cutting wood." The money they brought in meant the family had food—chicken, eggs, bread.

The fake ID cards protected them when the gendarmes [police], and later the Germans, came through the village looking for Jews.

But the family was in constant danger. It only took one person to call the police about the Jewish family in the village.

"Being as young as I was, I didn't realize that, but now I realize I could have been arrested at any time, and you know, sent to a camp at seven, eight, nine years old. . . . [N]obody [that young] came back. Only I think out of a million and a half children, maybe a couple of hundred came back and those were probably children that were arrested toward the end."

In one aspect, Henri's life mirrored a Hanukkah story. In that tale, Jewish children played outside of Torah study halls to warn the teachers and students of the approach of Syrian soldiers in the second century BCE. The Greek Syrian King Antiochus IV Ephinanes, whose empire included Judea, had banned many traditional Jewish practices. The study of Torah was punishable by death.

In World War II France, having a radio was punishable by death. "You could be shot for having a radio, but they had a few. . . . Us kids, we stayed in front of the house, playing in front of the house that had the radio. People would listen to the radio and we were supposed to tell them if we saw someone coming that we didn't know, police or otherwise, so they could hide the radio."

One reason for the radios, he later learned, was to send messages to members of the French Resistance movement.

"They had these funny, funny messages coming from England: 'Tonight is a beautiful night and the frogs are jumping.' That meant something to some groups. It meant they would send arms. It meant they had to blow up a bridge . . . It meant something."

Free French leader Gen. Charles de Gaulle also used the BBC to broadcast to the French people. "That's where we got the news because with the Germans, everything was fine, they were always winning. Of course, in the beginning, they were winning. But at the end that changed. That's how we got our news."

Outside of being a lookout, life was somewhat normal for the "Polish" child. "I was going to school even [though] . . . Jews were not supposed to go." After school, he would join other students in front of the building where they would play marbles and other games.

"My parents, my mother, always used to come and get me, and I'd say 'I want to play, I want to play.'" But he was told he had to go home. "I didn't know the reason for that, but they had a very good reason: They didn't want me to stay by myself. You know, you could be arrested anytime."

The fear was that the little boy would say something about being Jewish.

After being in Dun-Le-Poëlier for a short time, Henri's mother, Hannah, returned to Paris. She disappeared. "We don't know the reason why she wanted to go. She was supposed to stay a week or two and come back." After the war, he and his father found out she had been arrested and deported to Auschwitz Concentration Camp.

Henri's father, Ber, came back after his mother left. He had been in southwest France with the French army. He was part of a special unit made up of men who spoke Polish and Yiddish. At the start of the war, France had 550,000 troops on the Alpine front to guard the border with Italy.[11] But by June 1940, that force had been reduced to about 185,000 as the French sent troops north in a vain attempt to stop the Wehrmacht.

When the Italians attacked on the morning of June 21, the French no longer had the forces to stop them. Despite that, the Italians gained little from the fighting when France was required to sign an armistice with Germany's junior partner on June 24. Mussolini was not allowed to annex the territories he wanted, such as Nice. The Germans only allowed Italy to take French territory along the Alpine defense line, up to about three miles deep.[12]

Under the terms of the Italian armistice, most French troops were to evacuate demilitarized areas within ten days of the end of fighting.[13] At the start of the war, France had a 2.3 million-man army.[14] During the fighting, more than 200,000 French troops died,[15] while another approximately 1.8 million became prisoners of war. Some of the troops avoided prison camp. It was not

This is a photo of Henri's mother, Hannah Gudthajm. She disappeared when she returned to Paris soon after France surrendered to Germany.

uncommon for some of those soldiers to exchange their uniforms for civilian clothes, merging with the general population.

Ber Goodheim was among those who were not taken as POWs. He eventually found Henri and the others living in the little house the mayor had given them.

The family was not bothered by others in the village. Henri suspects it was because the area had many members of the Resistance, which brought its own kind of dangers. The Resistance fighters would try to inflict casualties or blow up rail lines or places where the Germans or French police would be.

"After each fight, of course, the gendarmes and sometimes the Germans would . . . arrest people . . . mostly men, as hostages. If there were casualties, they would kill some of them; if there were no casualties, they would release the hostages after a few days."

Among hostages who were taken were Henri's uncle, Jules Ratz, and a cousin, Simon David. Eventually, the hostages were released—except for his uncle and cousin and a man from another village. "They found out they were Jewish." Simon David and the other man were sent to Auschwitz where they died.

"But my uncle, I believe because he was a French citizen, was taken by police." Jules was taken to a field outside the village and told he was free to go home. When he got about ten paces away, he was shot twice in the back of the neck.

"We know that because the owner of the place where . . . this happened . . . saw what happened."

One Resistance strike led to an attack on the village. SS soldiers were on a nearby road heading to the Atlantic coast when the partisans attacked. But the French fighters had underestimated the number of German soldiers they would be confronting. Overmatched, the partisans fled.

In retribution for the attack, the SS burned all the farms in the area and started firing mortar shells into the village.

"Of course, quite a few houses were touched, [but] I don't remember if there were casualties. You know the houses in this village, the [stone] walls were about a half-a-meter [eighteen inches] thick. . . . The only part that was susceptible to damage was the roof. So after a couple of hours, this stopped. We really don't know the reason they stopped. They wanted to destroy the village. . . . But they stopped and went on to the west coast."

On June 6, 1944, American and British forces invaded Normandy and were soon joined by Free French and other troops. The Germans already had been driven from North Africa and Sicily, and Allied forces were slowly forcing the Germans up the Italian peninsula. Then on August 15, 1944, the VI Corps of the U.S. 7th Army landed along a 45-mile stretch of France's Mediterranean coast, driving elements of the Germany 19th Army north. The U.S. forces were followed by the French Armée B.[16] While French forces turned to liberate Marseille, American troops drove north as the Germans conducted a fighting withdrawal until the 36th Infantry Division defeated the Germans, capturing Montélimar, routing the German defenders. On September 7, an American combat patrol linked up to the French 2nd Armored Division, which was operating as part of the U.S. 3rd Army.[17] With the exception of isolated German "fortresses," France was essentially cleared of German troops by September 1944.[18]

"So we had survived."

Henri had an uncle who had survived the war with his wife and two daughters in a village about 125 miles away. Henri does not know how his Uncle Leon Meyerovitch, who was a member of the Resistance, knew where they were—they had no telephone or any other way of communicating. But his uncle, who had a car because of his status in the Resistance, found them and thought it would be better for Henri to stay with them until life in France returned to normal.

So Ber sent Henri to live with the Meyerovitchs while he returned to Paris. His father was able to reclaim the apartment the family had before the war. "We were lucky because the person that had taken it had given it back, which was not always the case. . . . [W]hen they arrested Jews or when they denounced Jews, they could take whatever was in the apartment or even take the apartment . . . or the business. So there was some kind of incentive to denounce Jews."

While his father sought to rebuild his life in Paris, Henri continued his education, eventually graduating from high school at the Cours Complémentaires de Courvilles/Eure.

While he was in school he didn't tell anyone he was a Jew—it never came up, and he was now in the habit of not mentioning it and was not religious. Then one day, he was talking to his friends at the school when another student came up with an announcement: A new student was Jewish.

"Everybody said, 'Jewish? Oh, we have to see him.'"

"I told them, 'I'm Jewish, too.' They almost fell over. They had never seen a Jew."

Following his graduation, Henri returned to Paris in 1948 to find his father. It was then the teenager learned the extent of his family's catastrophe. "We realized how many people were killed and how many were missing. How many family, how many friends, how many relatives were missing."

One day, he was lining a shelf with a Yiddish-language newspaper when a small item caught his attention—it was his mother's maiden name. The name was that of one of her sisters who was in Poland. She had survived the war by hiding with Catholic nuns.

"That's the only one that we know from Poland that survived. My father had quite a few brothers and sisters, my mother had maybe a couple of sisters."

Henri and his father were able to find her and meet with her once, sending her money and medicine because she was not in good health. She died a few years later.

In Paris, one of the jobs Henri held was for El Al, the Israeli airline, running errands, issuing tickets, and making reservations, among other things. He had that job for a little more than a year.

Then in 1954, he entered the French army, where he served for two years as an engineer, building bridges and working in mine detection. He was stationed in the Paris area. He missed the French Vietnam War that ended in 1954 with France losing its Southeast Asian colony, and was not deployed for the Algerian War, which erupted in 1954 and ended in 1962 with France losing the North African colony.

Henri came to the United States in 1958 with the help of his uncle, Max Goodheim, who had immigrated in the late 1920s.

"That's the only relative [my father] had really left," plus some cousins and nephews.

Ber had gone to the United States for a visit. When he returned to Paris, he told Henri he liked America. He encouraged his son to also visit. "See if you like it," his father said. "If you like it we will go there, we will go there. If you don't like it, you'll come back, and we'll stay here."

Although his uncle sponsored him, his visa was slow in coming. "I applied for a visa, a permanent visa; it took about two years to get the visa."

Finally, Henri went to the American Embassy in Paris to ask them to expedite his papers because his cousin, Milton Goodheim, was getting married in December.

"I stayed a few months. I found a job through HIAS [the Hebrew Immigration Assistance Society], I had friends, French friends," and was living with his uncle in Brooklyn.

"I wrote my father, 'Look, I'm staying here. He said, 'Good, I'm coming.'"

Meanwhile, Henri was now living with his Aunt Suzanne. Suzanne was another sister of his mother, who had immigrated to the United States and was living in Brooklyn's Borough Park neighborhood. When his father arrived, he moved in with them.

"My aunt had lost her husband . . . my father had lost his wife . . . they lived together, they came together and they got married here."

They are both buried in Israel.

While Henri has never become religious, his father returned to his Orthodox Jewish roots after moving to the United States. They

This American flag was presented to Henri Goodheim in 2018 by Gen. W.E. Cole for being a survivor in honor of the victims and survivors of the Holocaust. The flag was presented to Henri after he spoke to a military group.

were living in a religious neighborhood and Henri believes his father wanted to go back to his childhood roots in Poland. But Ber didn't become strictly observant. "He liked to go to synagogue."

Growing up in France did not encourage Henri to become religious. "The French are not that religious . . . we don't mix religion with the rest . . . What can I say? Passover? Hanukah? I never heard of that until I came over here."

Henri got his first job in the United States with the help of the Hebrew Immigration Assistance Society. The nonprofit organization found employment for him with Igmor Novelties, where he packed products for shipment. He stayed there for about a year before moving onto other jobs.

Learning English was not a problem. "If you know Yiddish, you have a feeling for English" because many of the words are similar. "Don't forget there's a lot of German words in English. . . .

Yiddish is also a lot of German words. . . . And then I had two years [of English] in high school."

In 1960, he enrolled in Brooklyn College, majoring in economics.

It was about this time that Henri met Lucienne Depres, the woman who would become his wife, through a mutual French friend.

"What is funny is that she lived in France about 15 miles away from where I was during the war."

They married on January 30, 1965, in Brooklyn. His wife had converted to Judaism.

It took Henri nearly ten years to finish his bachelor's degree because he was working a full-time job and going to school at night. Along the way, his children were born between 1965 and 1971.

"I went to graduate school for a year. But you know I had already gone almost ten years at night. You know, and four kids, a full-time job. I couldn't take it anymore."

The full-time job was working as a computer programmer after attending an IBM school. "I found a job with EF Hutton . . . which was not easy because, at the time, not too many brokerage houses were hiring Jewish people."

He stayed at that job for four years as a program analyst before going to work for an import-export business, Phillip Brothers. That company was bought by Angel Heart Mineral Chemicals, which in turn was bought by Solomon Brothers. Eventually, Solomon Brothers was sold to Citibank. Henri stayed with his job through all those changes.

He retired in 1999. His wife died that March. "So all the plans that we had, there's nothing to do . . ."

The Holocaust has been a constant throughout Henri's life. And it intruded in unexpected ways.

One day, his step-sister's husband was touring the Museum of Jewish Heritage in New York City. Simon Holeman was stopped by a picture of a woman and a child who died in the Holocaust—a picture of his first wife and their child. All three were sent to concentration camps. Simon survived six of the camps, finally being liberated when the Red Army captured Auschwitz.

Henri doesn't know how the museum came by that photograph, he only knows the deep impact it had on Simon.

Simon didn't want to talk about his experiences in the camps until a few years before his death. His grandson asked him to talk to his class during their study of the Holocaust.

And once in a while, he would talk to Henri. Simon, who was an electrical worker, "would tell me, you know, 'We worked on high tension wires.'" They would work in the rain or the snow, any kind of weather. If one of the workers was electrocuted, his body was "pushed aside, bring someone else in." Then the corpse would be taken away. "That was it. No big deal."

Until about six years ago, Henri did not talk much about his experiences during the Holocaust, either. He occasionally talked about it during visits to his wife's family in France.

"This is where my wife's family, her parents, lived, so we had to talk about it," especially since they were a short distance from the village where he spent the war.

"You know you can't just hide the whole thing. But it's not a question of hiding. It's just that it never, never came to mind to tell the story."

"But you know lately I've been more open." Henri has started speaking in front of groups, Jews and non-Jews, including school children and members of the U.S. Army, as well as civilian workers, to preserve the memory, the reality, of what happened.

And to combat anti-Semitism.

Today, slightly more than 14.5 million Jews are alive, most in Israel and the United States.[19] Meanwhile, the world's population has grown to more than 7.6 billion.[20]

Henri starts his presentation by asking his audience: "How many Jews are in this world?"

"And they don't know. Some would tell a hundred million. Some would tell two hundred million." Then he tells them how many there really are.

"I say we are accused of many things: We own Hollywood, we own banks, we own the brokerage house." How can that be? he asks. "They have no idea." So that is why he starts with the question: "How many Jews do you think there are in the world that we caused so many problems?"

Henri never was in a concentration camp, which is the only reason he, his four children, and six grandchildren are alive today.

"I'm 85. [But during World War II,] I'm a youngster. You have to understand that had I been arrested, I had no chance of survival. Children . . . would not survive at six, seven, eight, nine.

They only had a chance if you're fifteen, sixteen, and you looked healthy enough to work. . . . I could have been denounced and disappeared. I would have, there wouldn't have been anymore Henri Goodheim."

NOTES

1. Holocaust Encyclopedia.
2. Robert Forczyk, *Case Red* (n.p.: Osprey Publishing, 2017).
3. Hogan, *The Holocaust Chronicle*, 186.
4. Hogan, *The Holocaust Chronicle.*
5. Kathryn J. Atwood, *Code Name Pauline: Memories of World War II Special Agent* (n.p.: Chicago Review Press, 2013).
6. Atwood, *Code Name Pauline.*
7. *The Holocaust Chronicle*, 186.
8. https://www.history.com.
9. *The Holocaust Chronicle*, 197.
10. *The Holocaust Chronicle*, 186.
11. Forczyk, *Case Red.*
12. Forczyk, *Case Red.*
13. "Bulletin of International News", vol. 17, no. 14, 852–854.
14. Forczyk, *Case Red*, 238.
15. https://www.wikiwand.com/.
16. American Battle Monuments Commission, https://www.abmc.gov.
17. American Battle Monuments Commission.
18. StackExchange, https://history.stackexchange.com.
19. https://www.jewishpress.com.
20. https://www.worldometers.info.

"I went to bed every night and I prayed to God. I says, 'If I don't survive, God, please don't let me wake up. I don't want to be shot with a bullet."

—Tina Berkowitz

CHAPTER 10

SURVIVING ON THE RUN

Tina Berkowitz, formerly Tema Litman

In 1939, Kozienice, Poland, was home to about 5,000 Jews. A year later, 12,000 Jews had been squeezed into the ghetto. By the end of 1942, most were dead. Some had been sent to labor camps and a few survived by hiding.

But on December 1, 1924, that was all in the future for a newborn girl, Tema Litman, the future Tina Berkowitz, the second child and first daughter of Leyva and Mayta Litman. Her brother, Maurice, had been born three years before her. Her three sisters followed in three-year intervals: Rachel, Hanna, and Ita.

Leyva was a commodities broker who also had a small grocery store with his wife, the former Mayta Lipman, in the city about 58 miles south of Warsaw. Every summer, Leyva would rent orchards from locals Poles and ethnic Germans, bringing his family to the countryside, including Tema. "We were there for three months until the fruit was finished and we took them off, and returned to Kozienice."

In town, the family lived in a building which had their store on the first floor while they lived on the second. They had inherited it from Tema's grandmother.

Tema's mother ran the store. On Thursdays, Poles would "sell their wares on our street . . . then they came into the store and bought stuff from us."

When she was twelve years old, Tema started to help take care of the store. "I always helped in the house with everything, with cooking, with cleaning . . . in the store so much during the week, I didn't have much time for myself unless there was something going on in my school. Then I had to be there. But Sunday was a good day for me. I could go and play with my friends and go on picnics and all kinds of things."

"Growing up I was going to Polish schools with the Poles . . . and then when I came home from public school, I went to Beit Yaakov," the Hebrew school. "The town was heavily Jewish. . . . We lived among the Poles. Not segregated. Near our house was a [Polish-owned] bar, and across the street, also Poles." Some ethnic Germans also lived in the town.

But living together did not mean peace or even acceptance. "All of a sudden some of the Poles would go crazy, and they started up with rocks. . . . We had to up and close the shutters [on their house and business]. . . . Sometimes for twenty-four hours we couldn't go out of the house."

At school, Jewish students were frequently the target of attacks by Polish children. "We still went to the same schools. We had no choice." Teachers would make Jewish children come to the front of the class, and then examine their clothing for lice.

Tema didn't have Polish friends. "Not friends that you call friends."

Despite those problems, Jews were active in the town's government, including serving as town councilors.[1]

While the Jews had problems with the Poles, the ethnic Germans, known as *Volksdeutsche,* had good relations with Jews, but not with the Poles. They were known to beat Polish farm workers, take advantage of Polish workers, and resist the authority of the Polish government. When Poles declared a boycott of Jewish businesses in Kozienice, the ethnic Germans were the first to break it.[2]

In August 1939, as tensions between Germany and Poland grew and both sides began to mobilize, the ethnic Germans' attitude toward their Jewish neighbors changed. They cut off business dealings with Jews and would no longer respond to greetings from them.[3]

The Germans painted the chimneys of their houses red to identify themselves. And because the Germans' behavior toward Poles also became provocative, Polish authorities had all the German men rounded up and taken to the Bereza Kartuska security prison. On their way to prison, the Germans would yell insults at Polish officials and scream "Heil Hitler."[4]

Having swallowed Austria in 1938, followed by Czechoslovakia, German Fuhrer Adolf Hitler now had his army, the Wehrmacht, on three sides of Poland. Germany lay to the west and north of Poland, while Czechoslovakia, or what was left of it, was to the south. The only gap was the Polish Corridor, which gave Poland access to the Baltic Sea, but separated Germany proper from East Prussia. Created by the Treaty of Versailles in 1919 after World War I, the corridor contained the Free City of Danzig, which was mostly made up of Germans. The corridor's population outside Danzig was a mixture of Poles and Germans.[5]

Hitler was demanding the return of Danzig, as well as extraterritorial access to the city.[6] That excuse of bringing all Germans into the Reich lay behind the incorporation of Austria and the Czech Sudetenland into Germany. It now formed the basis for the demand which would lead to World War II.

The Polish government rejected the German demand, and the two countries began to move toward war.[7] The British and French governments allied themselves with Poland.

The Germans did not want to take the blame for starting the war with Poland. On the evening of August 31, SS troops dressed in Polish uniforms simulated attacks just inside the German border during the operation code-named Canned Goods. There were several fake attacks, with the main one at the radio station in Gleiwitz, Germany. Murdered concentration camp inmates, who also were in Polish uniforms, were left as casualties.[8]

The Wehrmacht crossed the border at dawn on September 1, 1939.[9] Britain and France declared war on Germany on September 3 after Hitler ignored their ultimatum to withdraw from Poland.

And Tema was taking care of the store with the help of a little Jewish girl who lived across the street.

A few days after the start of hostilities, Leyva, Tema's father, closed the store and took his family to the orchards he had rented

This is a picture of Tema's kindergarten class. She is in the front row on the extreme left. (Courtesy of Tina Berkowitz.)

in the countryside as a precaution, sparing them from the initial horrors of the German occupation of Kozienice.

The war reached Kozienice early on September 8 when the German air force, the Luftwaffe, bombed the town indiscriminately, just avoiding the houses with red chimneys. The bombing set buildings on fire.[10]

During that bombing, the Litmans' house was destroyed, killing all who were inside. "Most of my [extended] family was there in the house, and people when they heard the [air-raid] alarm, so they run into our house [seeking protection]. They got killed, too. My mother's brother, and two sisters. My uncle's [Avram Lipman] feet . . . were sticking up from the hole [left by the bomb]. That's how they pulled him out, about four people they pulled out." His two daughters also died, as well as five or six people who had run into the house seeking shelter.

This scenario was repeated in many houses in Kozienice as people sought safety from the bombs only to be killed in a direct hit.

To escape the bombings, Jews fled to the nearby forest, but not everyone made it because the Nazi's planes attacked them as they fled.[11]

Hiding among the trees, the Jews had no news about what was happening or where the Germans were. All they saw were routed Polish soldiers fleeing in panic, some barefoot, some without weapons. They were seeking to cross the Vistula River, four miles from Kozienice, in an attempt to escape from the Germans. Because the Luftwaffe had destroyed the bridges, the soldiers tried to cross in boats only to be attacked by the planes.[12]

A Polish officer stopped to talk to the Jews huddled in the forest. He said his name was Jozef Dembski. He told the Jews the Polish government had fled Warsaw and the army had collapsed. Then he committed suicide.[13]

The next day, a young man returned from town. He had gone back before dawn to see what was happening only to be caught by the Germans who asked him where the Jews were. The young man told them they had taken refuge in the forest to escape the bombs. The message he carried back from the Germans: If the Jews did not return to town by 1 P.M., the forest would be shot up. A debate ensued over what to do, with some arguing to return and others to flee toward Lublin with the retreating Polish army. A small group headed toward Lublin while the majority returned to town.

About 2,000 Jews headed back from the forest. As they entered Kozienice, they were surrounded by Nazi soldiers who beat men, women, and children with rifles and fists. The soldiers tore the men's beards off by hand or cut them off with bayonets, often slicing into their skin in the process. A young man with a hunchback was pulled out of the group and shot. Jews were then ordered to silently stand still, or be shot. The soldiers said they were searching for weapons, and took all the money they found. Men and women were left standing half-naked in the street.[14]

That evening, September 9, the Jews were driven into a church courtyard, where men and women were separated and again searched. The Germans took any money missed in the earlier search. Later, one of the men was taken inside the church and beaten nearly to death. He was then brought out into the courtyard and other Jews were ordered to dig a grave. The man was buried alive.[15]

The next morning, the men were formed up and forced to run; those who fell were beaten. After an hour, they were put to work sweeping the courtyard and cleaning toilets with their hands; they were forced to eat feces. That afternoon, the women and children were released. The Germans threatened to shoot the men as "enemies of the world."[16]

A soldier then demanded to know where the town's rabbi was, threatening to hang all the men if he was not turned over. The problem was that the rabbi had fled to Lublin with the group in the forest. Lacking a rabbi to hang, the Germans picked out the richest man, Shmuel-Moshe Korman, and hung him from a tree in front of all the other Jews. Before he died, they cut the rope.

When he recovered, they hung him again. And again. And again. Korman begged them to be let him die. An SS officer told him, "Dogs die, but Jews suffer."[17]

When his wife discovered what was going on, she bribed the German commandant, and her husband was released.[18]

After that, sixty Jews were taken into the forest and ordered to dig a mass grave for themselves. When they had finished, they were forced to lie in it in what became a mock execution. They then were returned to the courtyard. The Germans drove 2,000 Jews into one room in the church, keeping them there for six days, where some died for lack of oxygen. They were brought outside, attacked, this time by Polish prisoners-of-war, and put back inside. On the seventh day, they were lined up in the courtyard, and all Jews who were older than forty-five were beaten and driven out. The younger men were taken to a concentration camp, possibly in Radom, Poland.[19]

This is the world Tema and her family returned to when they returned from the orchards. "We had no place to live [since their home had been destroyed in the bombing.] . . . My mother had a sister, [Figa Spiegel], she was a widow and she lived on the next street . . . and she had an attic and it was empty so we moved into the attic." Her father than rebuilt their house on the ruins of the old one.

The Nazis' Polish campaign ended October 6. The Soviet Union had invaded eastern Poland on September 17, while Warsaw surrendered to the Germans September 27. The brief period of Poland's independence between the world wars ended with the new Soviet border at the Bug River and the western part of the country occupied by the Germans.

The winter of 1939-40 was frigid. "We had snow and frost in the house from the cold. It was unbelievable. I don't think we had heat."

During this period, the Germans ordered Polish peasants not to sell food to Jews, on pain of death. That sparked smuggling on a large scale and included bribing German officials to look the other way.[20]

"And, of course, when they made the ghetto it was a horrible life. We couldn't go out anymore from the house. People were already getting starved."

The ghetto was established in the fall of 1940 when 12,000 Jews from Kozienice and the surrounding area[21] were forced first

Tema Litman after the war ended. (Courtesy of Tina Berkowitz.)

into a fifteen-street area and then into three streets. A *Judenrat*, or Jewish council, was created with Hershel Perl as the chairman and Moshe Bronsztain in charge of the labor department. Bronsztain's responsibility was to pick who would work and who would be deported.[22]

Tema and her family, along with the other Jews, struggled to stay alive in this deadly constriction. "They started bringing in from other towns Jewish people . . . into the ghetto, and they were shooting in the streets or the court took somebody."

One day, Polish police and German SS demanded that Tema's Uncle Avram Lipman tell them where his grown son, Ichel, lived. Poles had told the Germans that Ichel had hid furs and leather that he was supposed to have turned over. When Avram took the Germans there, the two men were paraded through the streets and then shot in front of Tema's house. Her mother, Mayta, was then ordered to bury brother and nephew under the window of her home. Leyva begged the Jewish and Polish committees for permission to bury them in the cemetery but was rejected.

—

Forcing all the Jews into one small three-block area created health problems which the Germans solved by shooting anyone who contracted typhus, including a ten-year-old boy who was killed while his mother was having a prescription filled for him.[23]

The Germans also took quilts, blankets, furniture, and beds from Jewish homes.

SS troops would force Jews to clean roads and have them do meaningless work, such as digging pits and then filling them in. The Germans would photograph the Jews while they were working, ordering them to smile and laugh for the camera.[24]

The Judenrat organized daily work parties, ordering all men between the ages of fifteen and sixty to report every morning for work assignments. The Germans also ordered the Judenrat to organize a Jewish police force to keep order in the ghetto. Any Jew caught on the Aryan side without a special permit or a Star of David armband was shot.[25]

In early 1941, the ghetto was enclosed with barbed wire and a curfew imposed. Jews who were caught outside the ghetto were shot on the spot. But with food scarce, many took the risk, and many were shot.[26] Others died of starvation or from disease their malnourished bodies could not fight off.

"They didn't have anything [to eat] . . . so they were just dying, children laying, dying, and this went on and on."

Tema's teenage brother, Maurice, was one of the Jews who risked being shot to get food for the family. "At twelve at night, he took chances and he went to the peasants and he brought back whatever he could, food. But it came a time [in early 1941] when we didn't have anymore, all the potatoes were gone. My mother used to peel potatoes and cook the peels."

One day Leyva told Maurice to talk to a Pole he knew about getting out of the ghetto with sixteen-year-old Tema. "My brother somehow got in touch with him, and he said, 'I think I can help you, but I don't think I can help your sister. She's too young for that place that I want to send you.' So my brother says, 'I'll take my chances. She has to go with me.' My other sisters would never leave my mother. My father said to me, 'I want you to go and save yourself. We don't have a chance anymore, but you are young and we want you to go.'"

Packing their few possessions, the two siblings slipped over the poorly guarded barbed-wire fence at night. With the help of Maurice's Polish friend, the two ran through farmland until they reached a place where ditches were being dug. The Pole told Maurice, "I told you not to bring your sister, they're going to kill her. She cannot work in that place."

"But I did go and I did work in that place."

After work, "at night we went back to the barracks to sleep. Everyone slept in the same place. It was all open, the top was closed and the walls around were open. My brother was in a different place."

One day, while they were working at the ditches, police officers arrived in open trucks and ordered everyone in. Tema had been working barefoot in the muddy ditch, so when she began running across a field of newly harvested wheat, the stubble cut the soles of her feet.

Because of that and the fact "I was kind of tired," she fell behind the others and decided to hide behind a gate. "I was just sitting . . . and then I said, 'If they opened the door, the Poles, they're going to see me, they're going to shoot me themselves.' So I went back to the group and I run with all the others into the trucks."

The Jews were taken back to their barracks and told to run in, grab something, and run back out. Tema grabbed her shoes. It was at this point that she was separated from her eight-year-old cousin, Hinda, whom she never saw again. "They took her away. She was too young." Hinda's older brother had asked Tema to take of the girl because he was about to be taken to a concentration camp. She had Hinda with her for only a short time.

When Tema came out of the barracks, the trucks were gone. In their place were horse-drawn wagons. She and the others in her group were loaded onto the wagons. "Outside . . . there were Jews standing there. I don't know whether they work or from where they came, but this guy was from my hometown, and he saw me on the wagon." German soldiers were standing around with their rifles pointed at her and the others.

"This guy saw what happened to me and he ran to my brother where my brother was working. And all of the sudden, I'm sitting on the wagon and I see my brother. So my brother run to somebody, and he says, 'Please save my sister.' He said, 'It's too late. I can't do a thing for her. You can do whatever you want.'

"God is my witness, I still believe in God, my brother jumped over the fence. He pulled me . . . off the wagon and scraped me all over. And he says, 'Don't look back.' . . . And we ran and ran and ran until it was very dark."

They laid on the ground until morning. When they returned to the barracks, nobody was there.

Within a day or two, the Germans returned with another truck to pick up all those who had returned to the barracks. "They piled us all into that truck and they took us on the road. We didn't know where we were going; we were going day and night."

On September 27, 1942, about 8,000 Jews were taken from the Kozienice ghetto to the Treblinka death camp where they were murdered. The 70 to 120 Jews left in the ghetto were deported that December to the Pionki and the Skarżysko-Kamienna slave labor camps, although a few Jews managed to stay hidden.[27]

Tema and Maurice were among the Jews scooped up from work camps outside the ghetto. After their long ride, they found themselves in Skarżysko-Kamienna.

"We came in and I saw somebody from my hometown. He says don't say nothing . . . so I didn't say nothing. I didn't even acknowledge him."

Tema was in the slave labor camp named for the town which had a pre-war Jewish population of about 2,200. The German army occupied the town in east central Poland on September 7, 1939, instituting the anti-Jewish terror which had become common. The town's ghetto was established May 5, 1941, and in October 1942, all the Jews were sent to the Treblinka death camp to be murdered. A large slave labor camp was then set up, officially becoming a concentration camp in January 1944.[28]

In the camp, Tema was assigned to work with ten boys who were twelve or thirteen years old in a steel factory. She was making bullets during a work day which started at 6 A.M. and lasted until dark seven days a week. Each day started with the prisoners lined up for counting outside the barracks and ended with them lined up for another census.

While the prisoners were working, "they came around and watched you." If they didn't like what they saw, if the ammunition was damaged, "they took you out. You never came back."

While the factory made a variety of items, Tema was making ammunition until she was assigned a new job with a group working outside. "When the trains used to come with the steel, we used to take [the round steel bars that were at least five feet long] off

This photograph is of a group of survivors. Tema is the woman on the top right. (Courtesy of Tina Berkowitz.)

from the trains . . . and put them in the warehouses with shoes, no shoes, wearing *schmattas* [a ragged dress of poor quality]."

It was in this camp that Tema met fellow slave laborer, Hercko Berkowitz. He would later change his first name to Henry when the couple reached the United States.

The inmates were fed twice a day. "We got one slice of bread and sometimes we got a little piece of margarine" for lunch. In the evening, they received potato soup. The potatoes "were all like mushy . . . and the [broth] from it was like you make starch." Occasionally, the soup would have some meat in it. "They said it was horse meat."

Tema's diet improved when she was put to work unloading food, such as potatoes and ground grain, from trains. She didn't know whom the food was for, perhaps for the Germans. But it wasn't for the Jews.

The inmates who unloaded the food managed to steal some for themselves, and in Tema's case, she took some for her brother as well. He worked in a different factory in the camp. "I hid it and the next day, I walked to him . . . at lunchtime and I gave it to him and ran back to my place." She was able to get away with it because a Polish man who oversaw where she ate let her go.

About 15,000 Jews passed through Skarżysko-Kamienna between its opening as a slave labor camp at the end of 1942 and its closing as a concentration camp in August 1944. The surviving prisoners were sent to other concentration camps, mainly to Buchenwald in Germany and Czestochowa in western Poland. More than 10,000 Jews died in the camp from hunger, disease, or murder by the SS guards.[29]

The Germans closed the camp and sent their prisoners west to keep them away from the advancing Red Army as the Third Reich was collapsing from both east and west.

Tema was separated from her brother and Hercko as the camp was being closed. "They told us to get out of the barracks and get near the front gate where there were trucks." The inmates were lined up. The first group, including Tema, was taken to Czestochowa. Those further down the line were taken to Germany.

Facing the pressure of trying to survive, "we forgot about each other."

The Jewish experience in Czestochowa was a familiar one. The Wehrmacht had captured the city on the third day of the war, September 3, 1939. On September 4, the Germans murdered more than 300 Jews. A Judenrat was formed September 16, and the attacks on Jews and the theft of their property started. In August 1940, about 1,000 young Jews were sent to forced labor camps. Few survived. The ghetto was set up on April 9, 1941, and sealed off on August 23. About 20,000 Jews from such places as Lodz, Plock, and Krakow, as well as surrounding villages, were forced into the ghetto, which eventually held 48,000. After the murder of Jewish leaders and activists, the Nazis launched a large-scale action lasting from September 22 to October 8, 1942, sending about 39,000 Jews to be murdered in Treblinka. The elderly in the home for the aged and children in the orphanage were killed on the spot. About 2,000 Jews managed to escape or hide.[30]

About 5,000 Jews who were skilled and professional workers were left in the ghetto's northeastern area. On September 2, a German munitions factory owned by Apparatebau, a part of the Hasag network, was opened in Stradom, a suburb of Czestochowa. In June 1943, the Hasag Rakow steel mill opened. The largest camp in the area was the Hasag Pelzery, a munitions factory which had 5,000 slave laborers, while another 3,000 Jews worked in other munitions factories in the area.[31]

Tema was back making munitions and trying to survive the routine of standing in line every morning to be counted, working until after dark, and then standing in line to be counted again, all while receiving starvation rations.

As the Red Army drove ever further west, the concentration camps in the Czestochowa area were evacuated on January 16, 1945. Most of the Jews were shipped to Buchenwald and Ravensbruck concentration camps in Germany as the Nazi war effort entered into its death throes.

For Tema, "that's another story."

"When they knew that the Russians and the Allies were coming close, [the Germans] were very nervous. The Germans, you know, were like going back and forth, forth and back, and coming in. This was days and days and days.

"We heard shooting . . . we didn't know what's happening, but we knew something was happening. One day . . . we were standing for the count, and there's nobody there to count us. We looked at each other. . . . And we said, 'Well, what are we going to do now? What should we do?'"

They went to the factories, but those were deserted. "We didn't see a German. So we were standing there, frozen. It was so cold." The women had no warm clothes, only the rags the Germans has allowed them to wear.

"Everybody was saying, 'I think I'm going to do this. I think I'm going to do this.'"

Finally, Tema and about seven or eight other women decided to leave the camp. "What have we got to lose? There's nobody here. If they catch us, they should have shot us. . . . We were not far from the ghetto, and the thing is, there's nobody there."

The women formed a column of twos and set off. "We walk and we walk, and we look, and we hear shooting. We see fire. We don't know what anything is.

"A little bit away from the camp . . . we see a house." The women decided to try to get help. "This was already early morning and we were frozen, like we didn't feel [our] feet, nothing."

When they knocked on the door, a Polish man answered and asked them what they wanted and whether they were Jews. They told him, yes, they were. So, he repeats the question: What do you want? "We said we are so cold, please let us in, just to warm up a little bit. He says, 'What do you got for us? To give us?' . . .

We had a backpack. And I opened it up. I always look for soap to wash. I had a big piece of soap. So I said, 'That's all I have.' He grabbed it. Whatever somebody had, we gave him. He said, 'Come.' He took us away from the house, and he took us in where the horses were. We're in the barn. And he said, 'Lie there, lie on the floor.' Can you imagine what we had to lie in?"

"We said, 'You know what, we have to go, he's not going to give us anything." The women started walking again, thinking that they might be able to get into town. Eventually, they saw what looked like a police officer, but he wasn't German. Speaking Polish, they told him they were from the concentration camp, they had walked all night and were looking for a place where they could get warm and have something to eat.

The police officer turned out to be a Russian. He told the women to come with him. When they started to follow him in formation, he turned to them and said, "You don't have to walk like this anymore, the Germans are not here anymore.' We looked at each other like he's crazy. When did this happen?"

The Russian took them into Czestochowa. "We were walking on dead soldiers, on dead people frozen to the ground with ice between the eyes. And he said, 'Come on.'" They went up to a house and he knocked on the door. "This woman opens the door. She saw Jews. She said she didn't like it. He said, 'Open the door and let them in.' So we all went in and we sat down."

The Russian told the woman to feed them and give them a place to sleep. "We stayed during the day. . . . Then toward evening, the Russians started to come crazy for us. . . . We were hiding behind staircases" to avoid being raped. The Soviet soldiers were chasing women and raping any they could catch. "They are animals, the Russians."

After those soldiers left the area, "some of the girls that were with us went out. Only three of us remained in the house. . . . We went looking for food in empty houses."

During their search "in empty places to find some crumbs," they met an older Russian who spoke to them in Yiddish, telling them to come to him every day and he would give them bread.

Shortly after liberation, Tema and a cousin, Tema Oldtman, returned to Kozienice. "We thought that [we were] going to find somebody." They didn't. Her family was gone, and so was their house. In its place was a vegetable garden planted by a Pole who had been her family's neighbor.

Tema "Tina" and her husband, Hercko "Henry" Berkowitz. (Courtesy of Tina Berkowitz.)

Another motive for returning home was to escape the anti-Semitic violence in Czestochowa. As Jews returned from the concentration camps, from hiding, or from the Soviet Union where they had fled to escape the Germans, Poles were killing some of them. "The Poles killed a husband and wife in the street right in front of where we were living."

The two cousins did not stay in Kozienice long. Besides not finding anyone alive, the Poles there were killing Jews, too.

So they returned to Czestochowa and the precarious existence there.

It was during her search for food that she reconnected with Hercko. He had returned from Germany with a group of other Jewish young men. "Everybody was looking for somebody and looking for food or looking for clothing."

When Tema and Hercko found each other, "we never let each other go."

Tema also found her brother. Or, rather, Maurice found her. He also had returned from Germany. "Somebody told him, 'I think I saw your sister's alive.' So he came looking for me."

When World War II in Europe ended on May 7, 1945, with the formal, unconditional surrender of Germany, Tema, Hercko, and Maurice were in Czestochowa, three people among the estimated 10 million displaced persons. Some people had a home to return to. Others, such as Tema, her boyfriend and brother, had no place to go. "We wanted to go, to start going, to have a future."

Hercko suggested Tema write to his aunt, Molly Greenspan, in the United States. Tema and Maurice didn't have any family in the United States, which was critical for getting early permission to immigrate because of the need for a sponsor. Hercko wanted Tema to write the letter for him because he didn't know Yiddish, which is also called Jewish, very well.

"I wrote that Jewish letter to my husband's aunt. She was very poor, they were very poor. But they did everything in the world for us." His aunt and her family started working to get the documents they would need.

By this time, the trio was in Stuttgart, in the American zone of occupation, living in a Displaced Persons Camp run by the U.S. Army and the United Nations Relief and Rehabilitation Administration. They had ended up in that camp after meeting a distant cousin of Tema and Maurice who told them that was where she was going because she could get food every day. They went with her.

Tema and Hercko married on March 3, 1946, in Stuttgart while they waited for their visas. After being in the DP camp for a year, they left in March 1947 for Bremerhaven on Germany's North Sea coast to board the SS *Marina Marlin*. The American troop transport ship was built in 1945 and chartered in 1946 to the United States Lines and refitted to carry civilian passengers.

Crossing the Atlantic took twelve or thirteen days. After Tema and Hercko reached New York, they started using English versions of their names: Tina and Henry Berkowitz. Their aunt had fixed up an apartment for them next to her own. Their first apartment had no hot water and the bathroom was in the hallway. "It was sugar. It was just great" compared to what they had experienced during the war.

Her uncle got her a job at the Eagle Pencil factory which was about three blocks from the apartment. "I was black [from the graphite used in pencils] and with sores from the oil all over my body, and I prayed to God, 'Maybe one day I can leave that job.'"

After a little more than a year, Tina got a job in New York's garment center as a finisher. A finisher is the person who sews together the various pieces of a garment to make the finished product. It was piece work, meaning she got paid by how many garments she made.

"I didn't know how to hold a needle . . . but I learned with my eyes and my hands, and I became the fastest person . . . in the place. The Americans cursed me, and I was sitting and crying because . . . I took all their jobs away."

"I didn't work on a [sewing] machine, I worked by hand. Everything I did was by hand, and in the fancy schmancy stores we put our garments."

Tina held that job until 1954 when she went to help her husband run his business. When he first arrived in New York, Henry started to make specialty shoes for the handicapped. Then, he and a cousin opened a business making zippers. "It didn't work. It was horrible and he went out from the business. He lost everything.

"And then I went to help him. He opened another business. . . . I worked for this. Then he got sick." They had to give up that zipper business.

Henry eventually got a job with a business that also made zippers while Tina went to work for American Express processing orders.

During this time, their daughter was born in 1958. She would become a psychologist and "the joy" of her parents' lives.

After Tina worked for American Express for nearly twelve years, the couple both retired at age 62 and moved to Florida. "He felt he would like to come where it's very warm. It was a very hard thing for me to do because I had to leave my daughter" who was in New York.

Henry died in 1995 after suffering from cancer for five years.

As for Maurice, their uncle got him a job "in a notion place," that made buttons and bows. "My brother, after many years, he opened his own business. He did very well."

He married and had two children, before retiring to Florida. He died in 2012, a year after his wife.

When Tina was in Czestochowa, "I went to bed every night and I prayed to God. I says, 'If I don't survive, God, please don't let me wake up. I don't want to be shot with a bullet. This was every night that I prayed. I still believe in God. I always believe in Him. I wonder, 'Why, why the Jew was picked?' To people, my parents, my father gave away the last penny in his pocket."

Tina had another observation: "This is very, very important: I believe that it was meant for me to live."

NOTES

1. Virtual Shtetl Museum of Polish Jews.
2. The Destruction of Kozienice—Holocaust, 436, https://www.jewishgen.org.
3. The Destruction of Kozienice.
4. The Destruction of Kozienice.
5. Electronic Encyclopedia.com.
6. Shirer, *The Rise and Fall*, 464.
7. Shirer, *The Rise and Fall.*
8. Shirer, *The Rise and Fall*, 593.
9. Shirer, *The Rise and Fall*, 597.
10. The Destruction of Kozienice—Holocaust, 436, https://www.jewishgen.org.
11. The Destruction of Kozienice, 437.
12. The Destruction of Kozienice.
13. The Destruction of Kozienice, 439.
14. The Destruction of Kozienice, 440.
15. The Destruction of Kozienice, 441.
16. The Destruction of Kozienice, 442.
17. The Destruction of Kozienice.
18. The Destruction of Kozienice.
19. The Destruction of Kozienice, 445.
20. The Destruction of Kozienice.
21. Virtual Shtetl Museum.
22. Jewishgen.
23. The Destruction of Kozienice, 445.
24. The Destruction of Kozienice, 446.
25. The Destruction of Kozienice, 459.
26. The Destruction of Kozienice, 461.
27. Jewishgen.
28. Jewish Virtual Library.
29. Jewish Virtual Library.
30. Czestochowa During World War II, http://www.zchor.org/WWII.HTM.
31. Czestochowa.

"If I buy anything German, that makes me feel good because I'm not supposed to be here. I am spitting in Hitler's eye."
—JOHN GRAUSZ

CHAPTER 11

SURVIVING IN BUDAPEST

John Grausz

John Grausz was eight years old when Hungary became an ally of Nazi Germany on November 20, 1940. He was twelve when the Red Army laid siege to Budapest, where he had been born and still lived. The young boy survived because of his mother, who had "a spine of titanium," and his parents' Christian friends.

Anti-Semitism was widespread in Europe when John was born on October 6, 1932, to Leslie Grausz and the former Felice Singer. His father was born January 22, 1902, in Papa, Hungary; his mother, on January 29, 1900, in Nytra, Hungary.

War was not the only tool German Fuhrer Adolf Hitler used to expand the Nazi regime's dominance over Europe. In the case of Hungary, as with several other southeastern European nations, the Germans employed bribery. After the occupation of Czechoslovakia in March 1939, Hitler ceded the part of Slovakia and southern Carpathia Ruthenia to Hungary it had lost following the breakup of the Austro-Hungarian Empire after World War I.[1] Later, Hungary gained the rest of Carpathia Ruthenia, and in August 1940, northern Transylvania was transferred from Romania.[2]

Hungary declared war on the Soviet Union on June 27, 1941, five days after Germany launched its invasion of the USSR.

Today, John Grausz lives in Northern Virginia, after spending a career as a doctor taking care of newborn babies. The widower has two children as well as grandchildren.

John was born in the ancient Hungarian capital of Budapest, which is in effect two cities: Buda on the western shore of the Danube River is hilly, and Pest, on the eastern shore, is on flat land.

His father worked for a large conglomerate, NAK. The company's main business was coal mining, but his father worked in the cement division, which operated the largest cement factory in Hungary. As a Jew, Leslie was not allowed to be an executive in the company, despite his expertise in the business. "But he was high enough somehow that they would send him out to negotiate contracts, and things like that."

His mother worked as a secretary for an executive in the same company.

"There was anti-Semitism . . . but you could manage."

Things became worse in 1938 as Hungarian policies started to look more and more like Nazi Germany's. Anti-Semitic legislation was enacted in 1938 and 1939, limiting the occupations Jews could work in, reducing the number who were allowed to work in businesses, eliminating Jews from the bureaucracy and the news media, and ending their right to vote.[3] As in Nazi Germany, the laws were based on race and not religion.[4] Thus Jews who had converted to Christianity and their children also were targeted.[5]

John's father was able to keep his job, but his mother lost hers because one provision of the new laws was "only one member of a Jewish family could work at a company." Felice Grausz then became a partner in a small business dealing in heating materials and whitewash.

Then in 1941, "Dad was sent to a labor camp for two months each summer." Beginning in 1940, Jewish men from eighteen to twenty-five years old were conscripted into the Hungarian Labor Service; the age range was later expanded.[6] The Jews were made to dig ditches "which no one needed." But for the three summers his father spent in the camp, he was spared hard labor. "He ended up in the office because the camp commander was originally my mother's boss."

SCHUTZ-PASS

Nr. 14/22.

Name: Johann Paul G r a u s z

Wohnort: Budapest

Geburtsdatum: 6. Oktober. 1932.

Geburtsort: Budapest

Körperlänge: 142. cm.

Haarfarbe: blond Augenfarbe: blau

Unterschrift:

SCHWEDEN SVÉDORSZÁG

Die Kgl. Schwedische Gesandtschaft in Budapest bestätigt, dass der Obengenannte im Rahmen der — von dem Kgl. Schwedischen Aussenministerium autorisierten — Repatriierung nach Schweden reisen wird. Der Betreffende ist auch in einen Kollektivpass eingetragen.

<u>Bis Abreise steht der Obengenannte und seine Wohnung unter dem Schutz der Kgl. Schwedischen Gesandtschaft in Budapest.</u>

Gültigkeit: erlischt 14 Tage nach Einreise nach Schweden.

A budapesti Svéd Kir. Követség igazolja, hogy fentnevezett — a Svéd Kir. Külügyminisztérium által jóváhagyott — repatriálás keretében Svédországba utazik.

Nevezett a kollektív útlevélben is szerepel.

<u>Elutazásig fentnevezett és lakása a budapesti Svéd Kir. Követség oltalma alatt áll.</u>

Érvényét veszti a Svédországba való megérkezéstől számított tizennegyedik napon.

Reiseberechtigung nur gemeinsam mit dem Kollektivpass. ... wird nur in dem Kollektivpass eingetragen.

Budapest, den 21. August 1944

KÖNIGLICH SCHWEDISCHE GESANDTSCHAFT
SVÉD KIRÁLYI KÖVETSÉG

Kgl. Schwedischer Gesandte.

This is what is known as the Wallenberg pass John Grausz had that helped him stay out of Nazi hands during World War II in Budapest. Hungary was an ally of Germany during the war. The pass meant John did not have to wear a star of David on his clothes, allowing him to move around more freely.

Life for Hungary's Jews became precarious in mid-1944 as the Red Army drove the German army and its allies west, reaching the Hungarian border on August 23.[7]

Under pressure from abroad and with the approach of the Red Army, Admiral Miklos Horthy, regent of a Hungarian kingdom which had no king, had begun to resist Nazi demands that he deport his country's Jews. That did not stop the Arrow Cross, a rabidly anti-Semitic Hungarian organization, and others from attacking and killing Jews. And the Hungarians had been willing to transport Jews who were not Hungarian citizens to the Nazi concentration camps. Of the approximately 750,000 Jews in Hungary,[8] plus about 100,000 who were considered Jews under racial laws,[9] 762,000 were alive on March 19, 1944. When Hungary was liberated in April 1945, 255,500 survived either in Hungary or among those who had been deported. Nearly half the survivors, approximately 119,000, were in Budapest.[10]

On March 18, 1944, the German troops began moving into Hungary as the Soviet army was approaching from the east and Hitler now saw Horthy as an unreliable ally. The Germans began to move against Budapest's Jews on March 19, choosing 200 doctors and lawyers at random from the city's phone book and deporting them to Mauthausen Concentration Camp.[11]

On March 21, 1944, SS-Obersturmbanfurher Adolph Eichmann arrived in Budapest with a large staff of aides to work on "the final solution."[12]

In April, the Germans began to create ghettos throughout Hungary, eventually establishing forty, including three in the Budapest suburbs, and three concentration camps.[13] The facilities could hold 427,000 Jews at any one time. Between May 15 and May 24, 12,000 to 14,000 were sent daily to the Auschwitz concentration camp, with a total of about 116,000 men, women, and children going either directly to their deaths or to slave labor, which often ended in death. After making the countryside "Judenfrei," the Germans turned their attention to Budapest. Jews in the Budapest suburbs, plus some from concentration camps were put on transports. In less than two months, approximately 445,000 Jews were sent to Auschwitz.[14]

On April 26, 1944, the Swiss Legation sought to help Jews emigrate to Palestine, a proposal that was eventually taken over by the Red Cross.[15] That effort failed because of German intransigence. But the Swiss, Swedish, Spanish, and Portuguese consulates were able to put potential Jewish emigrants under their protection.[16] Palestine, which included present-day Israel, the West Bank, and Jordan, was controlled by the British who were restricting Jewish immigration to appease Arab public opinion.

On July 9, Raoul Wallenberg, a Swede who was the great-great-grandson of a Jewish convert, arrived in Budapest as a representative of the Swedish government, armed with a list of 630 Hungarian Jews who were eligible for Swedish visas, protecting them from deportation.[17] Wallenberg, who was not a diplomat, ultimately issued 4,500 protective documents, while Charles Lutz, the Swiss legate, gave out another 7,800. The Vatican issued another 2,500, while San Salvador gave out 1,600; Portugal issued 698 and Spain, 100.[18]

To protect these Jews, as well as another 700 who were trying to emigrate to Palestine, a series of protected houses were set aside for them, and Lutz declared the Glass House department store as an official Swiss government facility, protecting several hundred Jews.[19]

With the end approaching, Horthy sought to pull Hungary out of the war. On October 15, 1944, Horthy went on the radio to announce Hungary's surrender. German forces, which were already in Budapest, arrested him and installed a new government made up of members of the Hungarian National Socialist Arrow Cross.[20] Arrow Cross members immediately murdered at least 9,000 Jewish forced laborers.[21]

On October 16, members of the Hungarian fascist group, the Nyilas, were released from prison where Horthy had put them in July. They were armed and began attacking Jews. For ten days, Jews were prevented from leaving their houses for any reason. The Nyilas gangs also seized Jewish forced laborers, driving them to bridges over the Danube. The Jews were shot and their bodies were thrown into the river.[22]

Then on October 23, the Hungarian government announced that Jews with foreign passports or who were foreign nationals would be not be sent to Germany for forced labor.

As fascist bands roamed Budapest's streets, Lutz put 76 buildings under Swiss diplomatic protection, providing a safe haven for about 25,000 Jews. Lutz and Wallenberg issued more than 7,500 protective documents within a few days.[23]

But those documents did not always provide protection. The Germans, the Arrow Cross, and other anti-Semites frequently ignored them.[24] In one incident, the Nyilas forced hundreds of Jews into a brick factory where their protective documents were stripped from them, as were their valuables.[25] About 30,000

This is a star of David many Jews were required to wear in Hungary during World War II. But since John Grausz and his parents had Wallenberg passes they were not required to wear a star, allowing them to move around more freeling.

Jews were forced to march from Budapest toward the Austrian border as slave laborers. At least 7,000 died or were shot along the way, but several hundred were saved by Wallenberg and Lutz who went among the marchers, taking out people who carried their documents, and giving out Swedish and Swiss protective passes.[26]

On December 31, 1944, shortly after the Red Army had surrounded Budapest, the Nyilas blasted open the doors of the Glass House and started firing machine guns, killing three Jews before they were driven off by Hungarian soldiers.[27] On January 14, 1945, Germans and Nyilas broke into a protected house, killing twenty-six women, fifteen men, and one child. At the same time, attacks were launched against other protected buildings. Jews were taken to the bank of the Danube and tied in groups of three. The middle one was shot and all three were thrown into the river.[28]

It was in this chaotic, deadly environment that John's parents struggled to keep their only child and themselves alive.

His father and the ten other Jews, who were still working for NAK, were arrested by the Gestapo on March 24, 1944. "The eleven wives then went into high gear and searched for their husbands, and finally found them in a jail in Budapest, and followed them as they were transferred to a concentration camp in the Hungarian countryside."

The camp had two sections. "One section was [for] the transport to Auschwitz . . . [in] the other part of the camp . . . the prisoners . . . were held by the Gestapo. They were watched by the Hungarian police. . . . The wives were able to get care packages to them."

"One of [my] father's fellow prisoners did not like being held by the Gestapo, so he snuck over to the transport camp. He was never seen again."

John's father and the others were held until the Red Army reached Budapest when the Hungarian guards released the prisoners. "The Hungarians were anti-Semites, but they weren't murderous."

After his father's arrest, John was sent into hiding. "They sent me to stay with one of my father's colleagues," who shared an apartment with his brother, a trainee priest.

"I was in that apartment for a couple of weeks, maybe a little longer, but things went sour." John could not turn on a light or the radio, or make any noise so that neighbors would not know he was there. But he still had to use the bathroom. "The neighbors were starting to ask questions about when the two men were not at home, who was flushing the toilet."

"So, my parents took me home and they got me false papers" from a business colleague. His first name was the same as the dead child of one of the man's relatives. His mother's false papers carried the same family name; she was posing as his aunt.

"It got to be a bit tricky because when I was with her, I tended to say 'Mommy,' and that was like flushing the toilet when nobody was there. We had to be very careful about that."

At one point, John was sent to live with the sister of the business colleague. She lived outside Budapest on a farm near Lake Balaton. "Nobody bothered us down there."

"I got a very high opinion of cows' intelligence" while there. "She had a cow and . . . [it] was my job to take the cow" out to pasture twice a day. "I had to go over an old wooden-and-mud bridge that the cow was rapidly destroying. . . . The last time I took the cow over there, she sank in right to her utters, and just barely got to the other side. . . . There was a wooden bridge a little further down the creek and I brought the cow back" over that.

"When it's time to take the cow out to pasture in the afternoon, it headed straight for the wooden bridge, never broke a step."

Meanwhile, his mother was alone in their apartment. Budapest was being bombed frequently, but "she didn't want to go down to the shelter. So she was up on the fifth floor and a bomb fell in the courtyard . . . and just missed the [big stone] fountain and there was a thirty-foot crater. . . . After that, she went down [to the shelter]. . . . If that thing had hit the fountain, there wouldn't have been much left of the building."

After about two months, his mother decided it was safe enough in Budapest for John to come home.

"Things for an eleven-year-old . . . were not particularly exciting. I could go play with my cousin."

That lack of excitement didn't mean there wasn't any danger. "One day I was visiting my [maternal] grandmother [Bertha], and I was late coming home. My mother came to look for me." What she found was that everyone from that house was lined up, "about to march . . . off to oblivion. My mother had my Wallenberg pass with her so she pulled me out of line and took me home.

"We never saw my grandmother again."

In August, John's family had managed to get Wallenberg passes. "That was very helpful because, other than having to register with police every week, . . . you didn't have to wear the yellow star, so you could move around more freely."

Conditions didn't change for John and his parents until October when the Arrow Cross came to power, and then the Red Army besieged Budapest, reaching the outskirts on November 3, 1944, and breaking into the city on December 24. The fighting lasted until February 13, 1945, with the fall of Buda Castle Hill, bringing the battle to an end after 102 days, one of the longest sieges of World War II.[29] The fighting claimed at least 38,000 civilian lives, an equal number of German and Hungarian soldiers also died, while it is estimated that the Red Army lost about 70,000 lives.[30]

During this time, the family was split up in hiding as they sought to survive the attacks by the Nazis and Hungarian fascists, the shelling by the Soviets, the bombing, and street fighting between the attacking Red Army and the defenders.

"I had three places to be. Most of the time I was with my aunt, my father's brother's wife, who was Catholic. And we spent most of the time in an air-raid shelter. My mother . . . had a room in the neighborhood, and every now and then she would take me and I'd spend the night with her."

The third place, when "my mother decided that it was safe enough," was in the protected houses, where they would spend a little time.

"I don't know how my mother decided" where to stay. "I think she did it by the seat of her pants."

The bombing became so routine that at night the air-raid sirens didn't wake the family. If the bombs fell close enough, they would wake up and take shelter in the basement.

Ultimately, as the fighting intensified, John, his mother, and his aunt stayed in the cellar. "I'm quite puzzled by how we survived because you couldn't get out of the house, but we must have been able to, but I don't know how." And John does not know where they got food because "there wasn't any in the shops."

One day they did venture upstairs to his aunt's apartment. "There's a loud crash, they opened the door, and the next room . . . wasn't there. . . . A bomb went through from the roof to the ground. It didn't explode, but it just took out the whole tier of rooms. There was nothing but a hole."

During this time, his father's brother, Akiva Grausz, disappeared. "They have no idea what happened to him. He never came back."

Another uncle, Aldar Grausz, survived the Holocaust by hiding in the Hungarian air force, where he was a pilot. "He had more chutzpah than anyone," although how he hid he was Jewish is a mystery to John. During the war, Aldar got a German officer to visit his family to let them know that he was alright. The problem was: No one knew he was coming so they were unprepared when they opened the front door to find a German officer in uniform standing there, who gave the Nazi salute and said "Heil Hitler." They, of course, had to invite him in, and then listen, over tea, to an explanation of why Jews had to be exterminated.

"I never forgave [my uncle] for that."

After his father was released from the camp, he went into hiding with his sister and niece. A neighbor in their apartment building invited them to use a hidden closet with four other Jews. The closet was about three feet wide and ten feet long. "They had a big wardrobe in front of it." The back had been taken out but could be re-attached with clamps. "If anyone came to the house that was suspicious, they would scamper back into the closet."

Másol SCHUTZ-PASS

SCHWEDEN

SVÉDORSZÁG

This is the document used by Felice Grausz, John's mother, that helped her stay out of Nazi hands.

Then one morning, John, his aunt, and her niece were in the bomb shelter at his aunt's apartment house when they were hit by "what felt like an earthquake. . . . The plaster was falling off the wall and everything was kind of moving around."

He found out later that his father had narrowly escaped death. The Germans were using a schoolyard behind three apartment buildings as an ammunition dump. When Soviet artillery hit it, the dump went up. The school disappeared. The building nearest the dump also disappeared. The second one was heavily damaged

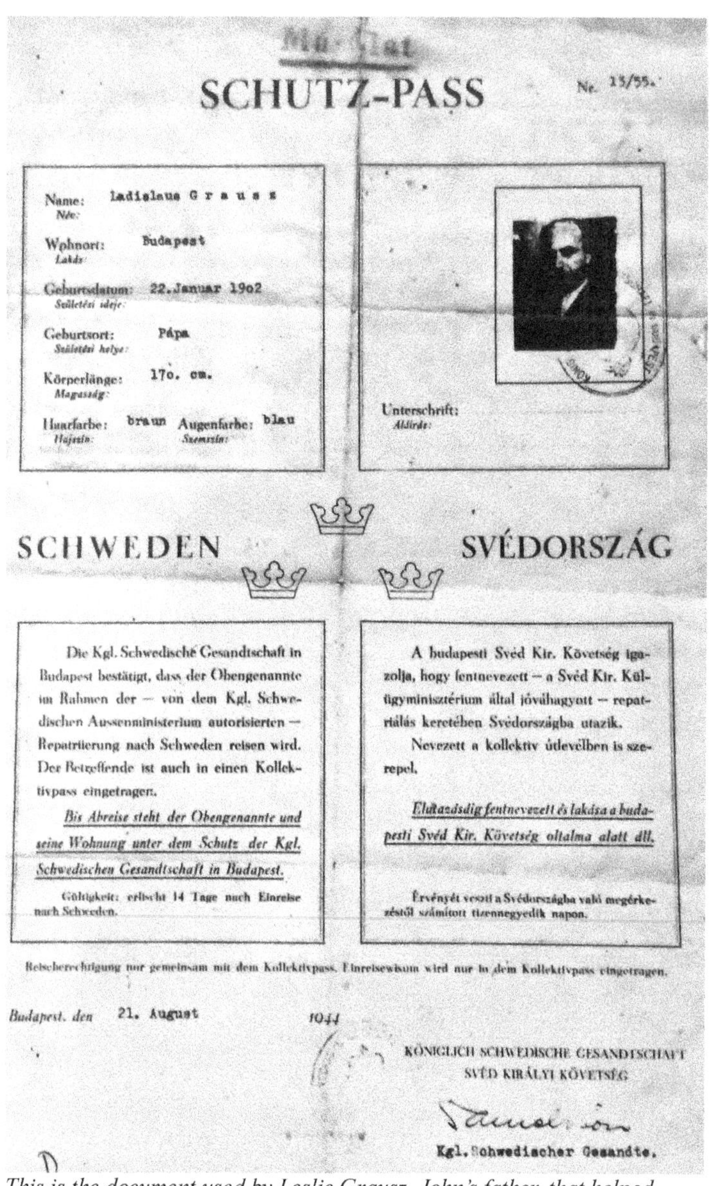

SCHUTZ-PASS

Nr. 13/55.

Name: / Név: Ladislaus G r a u s z

Wohnort: / Lakás: Budapest

Geburtsdatum: / Születési ideje: 22.Januar 1902

Geburtsort: / Születési helye: Pápa

Körperlänge: / Magasság: 170. cm.

Haarfarbe: / Hajszín: braun Augenfarbe: / Szemszín: blau

Unterschrift: / Aláírás:

SCHWEDEN SVÉDORSZÁG

Die Kgl. Schwedische Gesandtschaft in Budapest bestätigt, dass der Obengenannte im Rahmen der — von dem Kgl. Schwedischen Aussenministerium autorisierten — Repatriierung nach Schweden reisen wird. Der Betreffende ist auch in einen Kollektivpass eingetragen.

Bis Abreise steht der Obengenannte und seine Wohnung unter dem Schutz der Kgl. Schwedischen Gesandtschaft in Budapest.

Gültigkeit: erlischt 14 Tage nach Einreise nach Schweden.

A budapesti Svéd Kir. Követség igazolja, hogy fentnevezett — a Svéd Kir. Külügyminisztérium által jóváhagyott — repatriálás keretében Svédországba utazik.

Nevezett a kollektív útlevélben is szerepel.

Elutazásáig fentnevezett és lakása a budapesti Svéd Kir. Követség oltalma alatt áll.

Érvényét veszti a Svédországba való megérkezéstől számított tizennegyedik napon.

Reiseberechtigung nur gemeinsam mit dem Kollektivpass. Einreisevisum wird nur in dem Kollektivpass eingetragen.

Budapest, den 21. August 1944

KÖNIGLICH SCHWEDISCHE GESANDTSCHAFT
SVÉD KIRÁLYI KÖVETSÉG

Kgl. Schwedischer Gesandte.

This is the document used by Leslie Grausz, John's father, that helped him avoid arrest by the Nazis during World War II, although he did have to go into hiding during the war.

and burning. The third one, the one which his father was in, was damaged.

Because the building was now uninhabitable, his father and the others had to spend the rest of the siege in the basement with the other apartment building residents. "Fortunately, no one gave them away."

At one point during the fighting, John and his aunt were in her apartment on Csandy Street in Pest. On the street below, a Soviet tank was firing across the Danube at German positions in Buda. During the fighting, which lasted a few hours before the tank withdrew, the Germans responded mostly with sniper fire.

"And for us, about the 10th of January [1945], the door flew open and there was a Russian soldier with an arctic hat and sub-machine gun."

The fighting went on for another month, but John and his family were liberated. It was finally over on February 12, 1945, in Buda—the Soviets had taken Pest earlier—with the fighting being pushed to the hills of Buda.[31]

Budapest was in ruins. Virtually every building had been either damaged or destroyed during the fighting. Red Army soldiers looted and raped for days after taking Budapest.[32] The Soviets arrested people who were doing humanitarian work, including Wallenberg, who disappeared January 19, 1945, as he went to talk to Red Army commanders. His problem was that at least some of his work was financed by the U.S. World Refugee Board, which the Russians believed to have links to American intelligence. He was deported to the Soviet Union where he later died. The Soviets also may have believed he had seen documents related to the Katyn massacre of Polish army officers shortly after the Red Army overran eastern Poland at the beginning of the war in 1939.[33]

As for John, the end of the siege meant that his family was reunited—his parents, himself, his maternal grandmother, and his aunt and uncle.

"We all went back to the apartment where we lived before the war. It had been hit by a mortar shell on the window in my room." This was in January. "We moved into the innermost part of the apartment and sealed it up as best we could. . . . I don't remember when they fixed the window, but it must have taken quite a while." For heating and cooking, the family put in a stove fueled by coke, a fuel which is derived from coal.

It was still dangerous to be on some of the city's streets because of the continuing fighting, but that ended after a few weeks.

Eventually, John and his parents moved into another apartment which was less crowded. His grandmother and aunt stayed in the first apartment. The two apartments had one thing in common—in both, the room that was his had the window blown out. So he could only use the room in warm weather until it was eventually fixed.

His father went back to work for NAK, but now he could hold an executive position: He became the director of the cement department. The Soviets put his mother to work in a kitchen at one of the construction sites where the Soviets had impressed Budapest residents into service to build pontoon bridges and other kinds of temporary bridges over the Danube. The Germans had destroyed all the bridges during the fighting.

Food was a problem. So was heat.

NAK's main business was coal mining and it was winter. To get the coal needed to provide heat, the miners had to have food. To deal with that problem, the government sent out foraging trains into the countryside for supplies. Leslie Grausz was asked to lead the effort, which meant he was able to bring some food home.

"The young man who had hid me originally" was also on the foraging team. "When they got to a farm where they were going to start getting the food, they asked the young man what he would like to eat, and he said scrambled eggs . . . he ate 36 eggs. He was hungry."

Meanwhile, his mother began to train as a cosmetician in case she needed to work. And John went back to school.

When a provisional government was formed, the Hungarian Communist Party held a majority in the 495-member Provisional National Assembly. But in free elections on November 15, 1945, for the 407-member National Assembly, the Independent Smallholders Party won 245 seats, with Communists falling to 70 seats, to become the second largest party. The Smallholders held power until 1947. The party's officers were arrested and the party was eventually banned, and the Communists gradually took power.[34]

"Father decided he wanted to get out" in 1948. Leslie had a high school classmate who was a high-ranking official in the Hungarian Communist Party. His father contacted that friend about emigrating. When he was asked why, his father simply said, "I just feel I have to get out."

In an attempt to keep him, his father was offered the position over all the concrete companies in Hungary. That was something his father did not want. But he also had to be careful about his

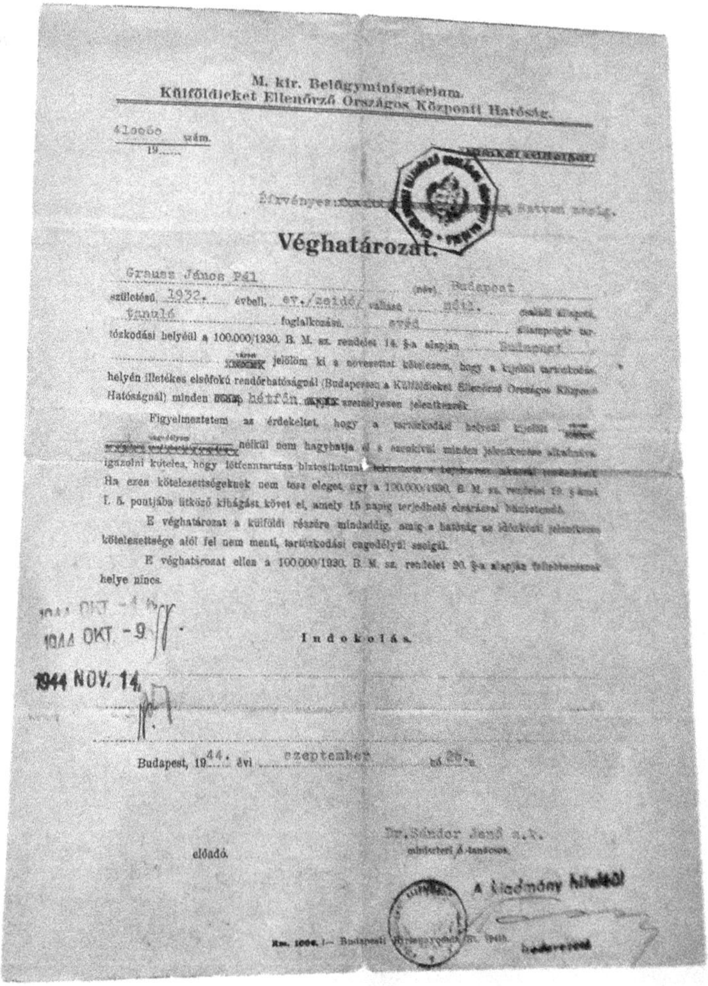

M. kir. Belügyminisztérium.
Külföldieket Ellenőrző Országos Központi Hatóság.

41oo6o szám.
19.....

Véghatározat.

Grausz János Pál [illegible] Budapest
születésű, 1932. évbeli, ev./zsidó/ vallású [illegible] nőtl. [illegible]
tanuló foglalkozású, svéd [illegible]
tózkodási helyéül a 100.000/1930. B. M. sz. rendelet 14. §-a alapján Budapest
[illegible] jelölöm ki s [illegible] hogy a [illegible]
helyén illetékes elsőfokú rendőrhatóságnál (Budapesten a Külföldieket Ellenőrző Országos Központi Hatóságnál) minden hétfőn személyesen jelentkezzék.
Figyelmeztetem az érdekeltet, hogy a tartózkodási helyéül [illegible]
engedélyem nélkül nem hagyhatja el s [illegible] minden jelentkezése alkalmával igazolni köteles, hogy létfenntartása biztosítottnak [illegible]
Ha ezen kötelezettségeknek nem tesz eleget, úgy a 100.000/1930. B. M. sz. rendelet 19. § [illegible] I. 5. pontjába ütköző kihágást követ el, amely 15 napig terjedhető elzárással büntetendő.
E véghatározat a külföldi részére mindaddig, amíg a hatóság az időközi jelentkezési kötelezettsége alól fel nem menti, tartózkodási engedélyül szolgál.
E véghatározat ellen a 100.000/1930. B. M. sz. rendelet 20. §-a alapján fellebbezésnek helye nincs.

1944 OKT. -9
1944 NOV. 14

Indokolás.

Budapest, 1944. évi szeptember hó 28-n.

Dr. Sándor Jenő s.k.
miniszteri [illegible] tanácsos.

előadó.

A kiadmány hiteléül:

Document stating that John Grausz is a Swedish citizen and does not have to wear a yellow Star of David.

reasons for leaving. So his father kept being evasive about why he wanted to leave and finally convinced his friend. They were able to get passports.

"And so we got on a train and went."

Their destination was Australia, where another of the ex-NAK Jewish workers had landed, and encouraged Leslie to come. Other family members also ended up in Australia.

John's parents lived on money they had brought from Hungary, but that did not last long. Leslie's Communist classmate had arranged for him to be a Hungarian import representative. So he and the other ex-NAK worker started importing jams and other similar products, as well as .22-caliber ammunition. "Rabbits were a big problem in Australia."

But just before the business became profitable, his father left it, worried the Australians thought he was a spy and were watching him. His father and mother then got into dress-making, a business they stayed in until retirement.

As for John, he was technically in the ninth grade but had missed a lot of school because of the war. Added to that was the fact that he arrived in Australia at the end of the school year.

"I got [to the school] the day before year-end exams, and the headmaster said, 'I don't know what to do with you but take the exams.' . . . I failed every subject, of course."

Among other problems, John knew little English and had not read the Shakespeare play which was on the final exam.

"The headmaster said that because I was six months older than the class, he'll give me a social promotion. . . . When I went back next year, I was far, far more successful," scoring in the ninetieth percentile in English. "That says a lot about their English."

After graduating from high school, John eventually went to medical school at Sydney University on a Commonwealth Scholarship. When he graduated, he wanted to specialize in pediatrics because "I like kids." The problem was that Sydney had one children's hospital, with four spaces for residents each year, and his medical school class had 172 graduates. "That was pretty prohibitive. So I was in adult medicine for three years."

Then a cousin invited John to come to Yale University Hospital in New Haven, Connecticut, in the United States. He spent three years there as a resident, entering the then-new specialty of neonatology, the care of ill and premature newborns.

He also found his wife in New Haven. He met Kathryn Netzel in 1961 at the hospital's front desk. The Pennsylvanian was a social worker, a natural born social worker. "People would just start telling her their life stories without her ever saying a word."

The couple had a daughter in 1964, who was born in New Haven, and a son in 1967, born in Boston.

After his stint at Yale, John went to Hammersmith Hospital in England "to get some English degrees, which I would need in Australia for what I wanted to do." He had applied for a fellowship there in the care of newborns but was told he would have to wait for three years, something he wasn't willing to do. But then two of the doctors who had received fellowships withdrew, so he spent the next three years working in England.

In 1964, he and his wife, Kate, were faced with a decision: Australia or America.

"I applied for the only [neonatal] job in Australia . . . and I got it. But it was in Melbourne, which I didn't know; I didn't know anybody in Melbourne . . . I knew of the people, but they didn't know me. . . . So I sent out thirty inquiries in the States and I got twenty-five invitations to interview, and we ended up in Milwaukee."

And John had received kind of an ultimatum from Kate. She said, "I will cross one more ocean." At this point, they had two small children, and they were going to settle in one country and stay there. "One of us was going home. My parents were in Sydney . . . her mother was over here."

He worked in Milwaukee for eighteen years and is still in touch with his former staff.

One of his high points happened about forty-five years ago. A premature infant, who weighed one and a half pounds, was delivered. This was her mother's sixth pregnancy—all were premature. The first five babies had died. This baby girl was saved because of the efforts of the neonatology unit in which John worked.

Twenty-one years later, he received a phone call—that baby had grown up and was getting married. And she invited him to the wedding. "We kept in touch for several years, and then we kind of lost touch. But four or five years ago we got back together, and now every time I go back [to Milwaukee] we go out in the evening and have dinner" with her daughter and her twins.

In 1985, John received a letter from a recruiter for the Washington Hospital Center in Washington, D.C. "They invited me to come at ten o'clock [in the morning] and at four o'clock I was employed." He became chairman of the hospital's newborn department, where he stayed until retiring in 2000.

John had decided he was ready to leave Milwaukee because things were getting too confusing. He had two employers: The Medical College of Wisconsin, which also operated a hospital, and the County Hospital. He had two part-time jobs but was expected to do three full-time jobs. The medical school wanted him to teach and be an administrator, the university hospital wanted him to take care of patients, and the County Hospital wanted him to get grants.

By moving to Washington, he had just one employer and one full-time job.

During his career, the one thing he did not want to do was deliver babies—he just didn't like it. "I delivered ten babies in my life. All of them in medical school."

What he did like was taking care of babies and trying to make sure they were healthy. "I had no involvement in obstetrics except to try to teach the obstetrician how to practice good obstetrics."

Another thing John didn't like was returning to Budapest, which he has done several times since the Communist government fell in 1989. "I go back so the family can see, can see what it is."

John also has returned to Europe for things like skiing trips. One of those trips brought a revelation.

He was passing through Munich about seven years ago on his way to a family skiing trip in Austria. He was walking down a market street when he noticed the "mishmash of ethnicities and races"—black, white, brown all mixed together, far from Adolf Hitler's Aryan dream of racial purity.

"The Nazis failed so abysmally it was just wonderful."

Something else also changed for John: His attitude about buying German products. In the past, he wouldn't. But now, "If I buy anything German, that makes me feel good because I'm not supposed to be here. I am spitting in Hitler's eye."

NOTES

1. Yahil, *The Holocaust: The Fate*, 183.
2. Yahil, *The Holocaust: The Fate*, 184.
3. Yahil, *The Holocaust: The Fate.*
4. Yahil, *The Holocaust: The Fate.*
5. Yahil, *The Holocaust: The Fate.*
6. Yahil, *The Holocaust: The Fate.*
7. *The Siege of Budapest* by Krisztian Ungvary, Yale University Press, 2005: 1.
8. Gilbert, *The Holocaust: A History*, 662.
9. Yahil, *The Holocaust: The Fate*, 506.
10. Yahil, *The Holocaust: The Fate*, 519.
11. Gilbert, *The Holocaust: A History*, 662.
12. Yahil, *The Holocaust: The Fate*, 506.
13. Yahil, *The Holocaust: The Fate*, 510.
14. Yahil, *The Holocaust: The Fate.*
15. Gilbert, *The Holocaust: A History*, 440.
16. Gilbert, *The Holocaust: A History*, 441.
17. Gilbert, *The Holocaust: A History*, 700.

18. Yahil, *The Holocaust: The Fate*, 642.
19. Gilbert, *The Holocaust: A History*, 701–702.
20. Yahil, *The Holocaust: The Fate*, xvi.
21. Yahil, *The Holocaust: The Fate*, 518.
22. Gilbert, *The Holocaust: A History*, 752.
23. Gilbert, *The Holocaust: A History*, 753
24. Yahil, *The Holocaust: The Fate*, 645.
25. Gilbert, *The Holocaust: A History*, 753.
26. Gilbert, *The Holocaust: A History*, 754.
27. Gilbert, *The Holocaust: A History*, 762.
28. Gilbert, *The Holocaust: A History*, 767.
29. Ungvary, *The Siege*, xxv.
30. Ungvary, *The Siege*, xxv-xxvi.
31. Ungvary, *The Siege*, 324.
32. Ungvary, *The Siege*, 139–140.
33. Ungvary, *The Siege*, 341–342.
34. http://www.globalsecurity.com.

CHAPTER 12

REMEMBER

No words, no pictures, no videos, not even a personal interview can capture the true trauma of what these survivors endured. Even for the very youngest who didn't really understand what was going on around them, these children had their lives torn away from them as they descended into the hell of the Holocaust.

Some lost their entire families, some emerged with some family, but all endured an experience which is incomprehensible to anyone who has not had the misfortune of having gone through it.

What is amazing about these children is not just that they survived the Nazi murder machine but that they held onto life in a world in which death was their constant companion, when they had no idea that the slaughter would ever end. And when the end of the destruction did come, they had the will to rebuild their lives, to start their own families, and to live on.

Today, when later generations look back on the survivors' experiences and the experiences of the six million human beings who did not survive, there is the knowledge which comes with reading the last chapter of a thriller: We know how the story ends before we even start to read the book.

We know the Nazis were destroyed. We know a remnant of the Jewish people in Europe survived. We know these ten children grew to be adults.

What remains for us in reading their stories is to discover how they survived, and to learn the meaning of hope in the face of horror. To get some sense of what they experienced, leaving us with a better understanding of what humans are capable of—both for good and evil.

We all face choices about what to believe and how to act. We can choose to hate or to love. We can choose to accept a fellow human being for who that person truly is, another human being who has as much right to walk on this Earth as we do. Or we can reject a person based on prejudices we have accepted as fact, seeing the other person as an object which can be rejected based on some surface perception which has no basis in reality.

The six million Jews, as well as the other victims of the Nazis, such as the Romani and homosexuals, died because of prejudice. Yet the survivors endured in the face of that unfounded hatred.

And they all emerged with scars from the experience, some physical, all emotional. Some, such as these ten, can speak of their experiences. Others cannot. Even more than seventy years later, the experience is too painful.

Some have kept their faith in God, others not so much. All have questions.

No one who has not gone through such an experience has a right to question how they emerged from the Holocaust. All we can do is learn from their strength, their determination to survive and to continue living. We, as people, as humans, can choose every day to be better.

And to pledge: Never again.

ABOUT THE AUTHORS

AMY Q. BLOCHER was born in 1950 in Miami, FL, the youngest of four. She graduated from Miami Edison High School there in 1968. She earned an Associate of Arts degree from Del Mar Junior College in Corpus Christi, TX, in 1970, a bachelor's degree from the University of South Florida in Tampa in 1972 and a Master of Education from the University of Louisville in Kentucky in 1993. She retired as a middle and high school teacher after a career spanning 37 years. She also has studied the Holocaust extensively, and taught about the Holocaust to both adults and students. She is active in Temple Emanuel in Lakeland, FL. This book is the fulfilment of her long-held dream to help preserve the memory of the Holocaust and honor those who survived and the memory of the six million who perished.

WILLIAM R. BLOCHER was born in 1949 in the Naval Hospital in Bethesda, MD, the third of seven. He graduated from West Springfield High School in Northern Virginia in 1968 and enlisted in the U.S. Navy two weeks after graduation. He was honorably separated in 1972 and graduated from the University of Missouri-Columbia with a Bachelor of Journalism in 1976. He worked as a reporter and copy editor in Michigan for five years, and then as an editor at newspapers in North Dakota, Virginia and New Jersey, ending his 41-year career in Lakeland, FL. He has studied history and the Holocaust both in college and since. Amy and Bill married in 1999 at Temple Emanuel in Lakeland, FL, and share five children and two grandchildren.

www.ingramcontent.com/pod-product-compliance
Lightning Source LLC
Chambersburg PA
CBHW021359090426
42742CB00009B/923

* 9 7 8 1 6 2 0 0 6 1 3 5 0 *